Kaizen Strategies
for Improving Team
Performance

In an increasingly competitive world, it is quality of thinking that gives an edge. An idea that opens new doors, a technique that solves a problem, or an insight that simply helps make sense of it all.

We work with leading authors in the fields of management and finance to bring cutting-edge thinking and best learning practice to a global market.

Under a range of leading imprints, including *Financial Times Prentice Hall*, we create world-class print publications and electronic products giving readers knowledge and understanding which can then be applied, whether studying or at work.

To find out more about our business and professional products, you can visit us at **www.business-minds.com**

For other Pearson Education publications, visit **www.pearsoned-ema.com**

Kaizen Strategies
for Improving Team
Performance

HOW TO ACCELERATE TEAM
DEVELOPMENT AND
ENHANCE TEAM PRODUCTIVITY

Contributions by associates of the Europe Japan Centre
Edited by Michael Colenso

Pearson Education Limited

Head Office:
Edinburgh Gate
Harlow CM20 2JE
Tel: +44 (0)1279 623623
Fax: +44 (0)1279 431059

London Office:
128 Long Acre, London WC2E 9AN
Tel: +44 (0)171 447 2000
Fax: +44 (0)171 240 5771
www.business-minds.com

First published in Great Britain 2000

ISBN: 0 273 63986 2

British Library Cataloguing in Publication Data
A CIP catalogue record for this book can be obtained from the British Library.

10 9 8 7 6 5 4 3 2

Typeset by M Rules
Printed and bound in Great Britain by Biddles Ltd, Guildford & King's Lynn

The Publishers' policy is to use paper manufactured from sustainable forests.

ABOUT THE EUROPE JAPAN CENTRE

THE EUROPE JAPAN CENTRE is part of the Osaka Gas Group, a major Japanese company that has global interests and information collection abilities that enable the Centre to keep up to date with the best management practices worldwide. We offer a range of services to organizations anywhere in the world, based around the twin pillars of human resources/management development and market research.

We have been in existence since 1991, and have gained an excellent reputation in a broad cross-section of sectors, including public and private organizations, large companies and SMEs, and industrial, commercial and service organizations.

Human Resources Development

Within the human resources area, the Europe Japan Centre focuses on the management of change, based on team development and the concept of *Kaizen* (continuous improvement). We are fortunate to have had in our team one of the last remaining members of Dr Deming's team, who worked with Deming for ten years in Japan and was therefore at the forefront of the whole quality movement.

'The best of East and West' is our philosophy, and our research department constantly gathers best practice information for us to use in our consultancy work. We are geared to achieving practical results. Our educational programmes are based on ideas and techniques which have been shown to work. By letting managers see how they can close the gap between concepts and action, we can help to change attitudes and to create an environment where people become more self-motivated, thus helping to bring about a more effective and innovative organization.

Our human resources consultancy offers:

- **Top quality seminars and workshops,** led by experts in their own fields of knowledge, or by experienced HR consultants who can put across their ideas in a clear and stimulating manner. Topics evolve continuously, reflecting our position as a leading consultancy aware of the latest trends in management thinking and practice, not only in the UK but worldwide.

- **In-house training programmes**: we have worked with a wide variety of companies to help them introduce new ways of working, including the introduction of *Kaizen* techniques, team-working, strategies for innovation, etc. Programmes can be short and concentrated or spread over a number of months or even years. Typical projects include initial work with senior management, followed by workshops, practical sessions and training the trainers.

- **World class speakers**: we can provide a range of speakers with the 'added extra' – whether from business, or the worlds of sport, entertainment or the media – to give an event excitement and make it live longer in the minds of audiences.

- **Event management and administration**: we are happy to work as the marketing arm of organizations by arranging seminars, conferences or other events. Our staff understand the importance of treating each organization's clients as we would do our own – as very special people.

Research

The second main area of the Europe Japan Centre's business is research. We focus mainly on market research either to assist European companies to enter and operate successfully in Japan and China, or to help Japanese companies within European markets. Our network of researchers in Europe and Asia means we have access to the latest on-the-spot information, and that we can conduct surveys or give advice rapidly and accurately.

For more information or to arrange an informal meeting, please contact Pat Wellington or Catherine Davis at:

The Europe Japan Centre plc, Mutual House, 70 Conduit Street, London W1R 9TQ; tel: 44 (0) 207 287 8605; fax: 44 (0) 207 287 8607; email: *info@ejc.co.uk*

Or consult our website: *http://www.ejc.co.uk*

ABOUT THE CONTRIBUTORS

EACH OF THE CONTRIBUTORS TO this book is an associate of the Europe Japan Centre and can be contacted through the Centre. All associates bring to the Centre's clients a mixture of line management experience on the one hand, and change programme developmental capability on the other. Associates are all competent consultants and most are also well known public speakers handling master classes and workshops on behalf of the Europe Japan Centre's clients.

Alan Barratt

Dr Barratt's particular area of expertise is developing teams at the most senior level. A former Vice President of Mobil Corporation's International Consulting Service he has worked all over the world. His chapter deals with the future role and needs of teams and teaming as we enter the next millennium.

Bob Bryant

An engineer by profession, Bob now specializes in developing open and trusting relationships in teams and in work units. As a former CEO of two National Health Trusts, and a former telecoms man, Bob's line management experience is considerable as the case study material in his chapter demonstrates.

Michael Colenso

Mike works primarily in the areas of strategy development and implementation. He has held Chief Executive roles in publishing, in training and education, and was latterly the CEO of the Open College. Mike has contributed two chapters, the first exploring the commonalities between Western team development theories and *Kaizen*, the second on the changing strategic environment in which teams will increasingly work.

Niall Foster

Niall's primary specialism is developing the organization's human resources to support strategy and to develop competitive advantage. He works in the area of teams and team building, in leadership and in change management. His rousing chapter offers solid inspirational advice on setting up the *Kaizen* team.

John Hall

A former director of the Centre for Leadership in Cambridge, John specializes in providing what he describes as simple and practical management techniques to release the potential of people at work. John's chapter lays out valuable diagnostic and alignment tools which help to get teams back on track.

Robert Hersowitz

Bob is a well known speaker and consultant. He specializes in designing and delivering programmes for organizational development in both the public and private sectors. Contributing two highly practical chapters in this book, the first on self managing teams, the second on virtual teams, Bob shares his broad, hands-on developmental experience with practical advice based on proven experience.

Christine Patrick

Chris Patrick is Director of the Europe Japan Centre. She has over twenty years' experience of working with Japanese companies, mainly in the research and training fields. She has lived and worked in Tokyo, as well as in Paris, Berlin and London, assisting organizations in creating multi-cultural workforces and in doing business globally.

Pat Wellington

Pat manages the Human Resource division of the Europe Japan Centre. She is an internationally respected specialist on *Kaizen* and besides the two chapters she has contributed to this book, she has also written a definitive book on *Kaizen* and Customer Care. Pat's contribution to the book is an explanation of *Kaizen* for those less familiar with it, and a chapter on leading the *Kaizen* team.

Annie Zlotnick

Annie's background is in education and in counselling. She has extensive experience in the health service environment but she has worked across a wide range of industries. Annie's chapter deals with teams under stress and offers excellent advice on managing this frequently occurring problem.

CONTENTS

CHAPTER 6

Self Management and the Kaizen Team – Empowerment versus Tasking 87

ROBERT HERSOWITZ

CHAPTER 7

Kaizen Teams are HOT – Honest, Open and Trusting 107

BOB BRYANT

PART FOUR   KAIZEN TEAMS IN THE FUTURE

PREFACE

THIS BOOK FOLLOWS THREE EARLIER works on *Kaizen* (see the end of this preface) which have achieved success around the world. When Financial Times Prentice Hall, the publishers, approached the Europe Japan Centre to expand the *Kaizen* list we thought long and hard about what to offer.

Kaizen is, of course, a Japanese management system which grew out of the quality movement. It has been widely adopted in the West but, more importantly, it has influenced a great deal of Western management thinking, especially in the areas of quality, process improvement and customer satisfaction. It seemed to us that there were two main areas where the practical utility of *Kaizen* would help the English-speaking manager: developing teams; and effecting organizational change. This book deals with teams; a further book deals with change.

Using teams as the organizational and operational components of the organization is becoming the rule rather than the exception. Application is wide and experience is varied. To try and span the breadth of the subject, we decided that a contributor book, with a number of the Centre's associates sharing their experience, would have more to offer the reader. We felt that this would give multiple perspectives on teams and it has turned out to be a good decision for the book is rich in advice, practical checklists of what to do, pitfalls to avoid, and case studies of success and failure.

We have organized the book into four parts which we felt would correspond to the sort of broad questions the reader would ask. These parts are:

Kaizen **and Teams** – which spells out the basic principles of *Kaizen* and indicates how it has changed, developed and continues to develop as it is applied around the world. We show also the relationships between research on team development in the West with the underpinning philosophies of *Kaizen*.

Setting up and Running the *Kaizen* Team is the second part and the four constituent chapters are the heart of the book. In this section we deal with how the team should be led, how set up, how transformed into a self-managing entity, and finally how best to develop the honesty and openness which characterize *Kaizen* teams.

Dealing with Problems is a shorter, two chapter section which offers advice on dealing with teams which are not performing as well as they could or have become stuck. Most managers will have confronted these difficulties and we offer some practical advice on realigning teams and on dealing with stress.

Kaizen **Teams in the Future** – this plots what we feel are likely requirements of *Kaizen* teams in the new millennium. We deal with their support of changing organizational strategy, with the virtual team – one where members rarely or never meet together, and finally with the need to enhance the learning capability of teams.

The purpose of this book is to show how we have taken the fundamental concept of *Kaizen*, and how we have each developed a variety of approaches to help organizations create a more supportive, creative environment. This could be, for example, through the work that Bob Bryant has undertaken in developing HOT (honest, open and trusting) interpersonal relationships, or the mapping work developed by John Hall. Each chapter has a unique perspective, and all of our consultants have developed their approach through hands-on experience in the marketplace.

In planning and in writing the book we have tried to keep in mind a vision of the potential reader. We see you as a busy line manager trying to get the best from your people and requiring fast access to pragmatic information and proven experience. We imagine you will dip in and out of the book as you need to. We imagine you might read it from the index rather than from the list of contents. We imagine you will not have a great deal of time to spare and we have felt that we should provide experience from which to select your own options for action.

The Europe Japan Centre is a consultancy. Besides our books, of which we are rather proud, we can also offer a wealth of advice and help as you build your own teams. You have the advantage then of reading about what we have done and how we did it as a precursor to seeking our help.

M. Colenso
Editor

Earlier books on *Kaizen* developed by the Europe Japan Centre and published by Financial Times Prentice Hall in 1995 are:

Barnes: *Kaizen Strategies for Successful Leadership*
Cane: *Kaizen Strategies for Winning Through People*
Wellington: *Kaizen Strategies for Customer Care.*

PART ONE

Kaizen and Teams

CHAPTER 1

Instant Kaizen – What it is and How it Works

Introduction

The *Kaizen* Environment

The Bigger Picture

Implementing *Kaizen*

Using *Kaizen* as a Springboard

Summary

PATRICIA WELLINGTON

Manager, Europe Japan Centre

For those unfamiliar with Kaizen, this chapter describes the *Kaizen* environment and goes on to explore those qualities which best characterize it. The chapter draws heavily on examples of good practice in the implementation of quality, continuous improvement and on customer focus.

INTRODUCTION

Kaizen, which we refer to as continuous improvement, means *change* and *good*. In a management sense this means continual and gradual improvements through evolution rather than revolution. The reality is you can make improvements once if you try; you can only make them more than once if you care.

It moves from the idea that 'If it ain't broke don't fix it', to 'If it ain't broke don't ignore it because it will break one day'.

- Bad business ignores the signs of disaster.
- Good business spots the signs of disaster and deals with them.
- *Kaizen* business constantly reviews and monitors to preclude disaster.

In a traditional business, re-examination is a project. Within an organization that has adopted *Kaizen* it is a whole way of life. People normally think of *Kaizen* as being applicable to a production environment and linked to monitoring systems and JIT. For the last seven years we at the Europe Japan Centre have explored in depth the whole culture and values element that needs to be in place for continuous improvement to be truly embedded into an organization.

The key concepts of continuous improvement are the bedrock that needs to be in place for other methodologies to work. However, with the ever-demanding needs of the customer and the changes in the whole way that organizations are marketing their services and products, there is a need for companies to be far more responsive to market trends. Not only should there be incremental improvement, but also breakthrough projects need to be used, for example, to bring a new product to the marketplace, create a different approach to offering added value service, or even in the broader context of helping an organization reinvent itself.

In this chapter I am going to be looking at the following:

- **The *Kaizen* Environment**
  What is the culture and values shift required for *Kaizen* to work?

- **The Bigger Picture**

  The organizational structure required, the responsibilities of management, the need for a sense of purpose through a mission/vision, and the overriding drive for customer focus company wide.

- **Implementation**

  In realistic terms, how do you start to introduce *Kaizen*?

- **Using *Kaizen* as a Springboard**

  Once the right culture, overall framework, tools and people are in place, you have an ideal springboard for breakthrough projects to keep your company at the cutting edge of developments worldwide.

So, starting at the bedrock stage that I have described above, continuous improvement is about creating an environment where people feel needed, supported and valued as individuals. You cannot force people to come up with ideas for improvement. You need to create an environment where people can have a sense of pride in their work, where they can feel that their ideas and suggestions are listened to, that feedback is given, not only for those ideas that are implemented but also when they are not. Reward and recognition are obviously part of the equation, but also the right to take risks and experiment without fear of retribution if things go wrong. Personal development and multi-skilling are other vital ingredients that make people feel that your organization cares about them as individuals, and which in turn will encourage them to want to contribute more.

People in their private life will often use great creativity, be it in gardening, home decorations, or photography. And yet how often does that creativity get transferred into the workplace? I do not believe that people come to work to do a bad job. It is your responsibility as management to create a company where people can grow and flourish.

It is your responsibility as management to create a company where people can grow and flourish.

So let us look at what it takes.

THE KAIZEN ENVIRONMENT

Openness

Openness in a *Kaizen* culture manifests itself in two ways: through the infrastructure of the building itself, and in interpersonal relationships.

Office space will usually be open plan, with individual offices only be for the most senior members of management, or acting as meeti rooms. There is a distinct lack of status symbols, such as car park spaces being reserved for key personnel, or separate dining rooms.

Unisys have developed this concept comprehensively and well in the form of Business Centres throughout the UK. In these Centres no one has their own personal desk, but operates out of a large locker space. For routine work there is an open plan area with PCs and administration support personnel. The area immediately around the administration area is inclined to be noisy, as telephones are being answered, and there is discussion around work projects. Should a member of staff require a quieter area for concentration, then they can book a PC at the furthest end of the room away from this area. For those who require total peace and quiet, for example if they are involved in writing a major tender document, there is a completely separate floor with individual offices. Attached to these offices is another administration resource, which is able to source and research specific information required for personnel working on this floor.

In interpersonal relationships there is also a constant quest for openness. As Deming put it, success is about driving fear out of the organization. It is about causing everyone's opinion to be valued, and removing the threat from minority views. Within this environment there is an open acknowledgement that in every-day corporate activity problems exist. It is important that they are not swept under the carpet, or simply put through to the Customer Services department to be addressed in a fire-fighting way. There is a need for root cause analysis to be undertaken to understand why problems have occurred in the first place, followed by cross-functional activity, if appropriate, to systematically address the issues. Persistence is the key, asking 'why' five times until you get to the cause.

Harmony

In Japanese culture the concept of harmony is of great importance. When Sir Edmund Hillary and Tensing were the first to climb Everest in 1953, the papers in the USA and UK reported Everest as being 'conquered'. In Japan the news was reported as 'Everest befriended'. In a Western environment the achievement was seen as conquering against the odds. In Japan the mountain was seen as aloof and needing to be befriended.

This 'befriending, harmonious approach' transfers itself into corporate activity, and will manifest itself through non-adversarial communication and avoidance of interpersonal confrontation. This approach will often frustrate Western managers when they are negotiating with the Japanese, since there are not only language difficulties to overcome, but also cultural considerations.

Clearly, a pragmatic approach needs to be adopted in an environment that has traditionally had a western focus.

The harmonious element, however, can be put into effect through sufficient cross-functional activity, secondment, or staff spending an agreed time frame in another unit with which they regularly have to have contact.

Inform

The vision and strategies of the organization need to be communicated on a regular basis, and must excite people by connecting to their values.

The word 'inform' does not just mean to *tell* people information, but to put it into context. It is important to ensure that your staff not only understand the facts but also the implications and the context of the information that you are supplying. Should you, for example, be presenting facts and figures, then your people need to have been given basic financial training in order to be able to interpret the information. The statistics also need to be produced in a user-friendly way.

It is important to ensure that your staff not only understand the facts but also the implications and the context of the information that you are supplying.

Very often I visit organizations that display their results for staff to see. The statistical information will often be produced in figure format, and laid out on paper that has started to curl over and look rather like tired cheese sandwiches! On a client site that I visited recently in the USA called Norriseal, Wade Wnuk, the President, had produced all the pertinent information with regard to shipping, distribution, and production in a graph format and had put small personal observations against some of the pie charts. This really brought all the information to life and made far more sense to the staff who were reading it.

Information is rather like a lift, it only works well if it goes up as well as down. It is management's responsibility to ensure that the information doesn't come up through filters and down through megaphones.

Information is rather like a lift, it only works well if it goes up as well as down.

Learning environment

In a *Kaizen* culture everyone is involved in the learning process, whereas very often in a traditional Western organization it will be purely the senior management and middle managers who receive the training and development. Training will be as and when required, rather than on a blanket basis, and will often be undertaken at a more localized level by a team leader/facilitator. Education will not only be task related but also include communication skills and team-building activities.

Training will often be the first thing to be cut during periods of recession in business. Organizations such as Nissan which have adopted the principles of continuous improvement have continued to train their staff even if there is a downturn in the economy.

A learning environment encourages every form of personal development, and organizations such as Mars Confectionery and Shell have learning resources in place for many forms of leisure activities. One of our clients, Braitrim, a successful small business who make coat hangers for Marks & Spencer, offers all their staff foreign language tuition in their lunch breaks.

Enablement/empowerment

True enablement/empowerment cannot happen unless people have been given the tools to do the task or job effectively. In many instances comprehensive communication of the objectives is sufficient, but often people will need training, be it on the job or off the job, to be able to move forward. Delegation with authority is vital, plus encouragement, feedback and reward. The Chinese Proverb below summarizes the process well:

Tell me and I will forget.
Show me and I may remember.
Involve me and I will understand.

Empowerment is not about getting employees to do what you want done, it is about getting out of the way so that they can do what is needed.

Empowerment is not about getting employees to do what you want done, it is about getting out of the way so that they can do what is needed.

There are clearly certain areas where empowerment is not appropriate, and each organization will have guidelines in place that are non-negotiable. This might be in the area of safety, finance, legality or security. The aim, however, is always to move from the 'granting of permission' stage through individuals communicating their actions and finally to total empowerment.

In talking about enablement/empowerment there is always a delicate people management element involved. If you create too much *people* focus with too much concern for people's feelings and personal problems, the result can be non-focused meetings or discussions, and the group always trying to do things by consensus decision. Ultimately this will mean poor productivity, no milestones being met, and items very often being repeated or deadlines being continually extended.

The antithesis of this however, is to have a too *task driven* style of management. This could manifest itself as pushing for results too soon, and too much concern for time and efficiency. The result that this will have on your team will be little creative thinking, concerns being ignored, and limited participation of some team members during group discussion. This will therefore mean discussions being dominated by the few, and decisions based on opinion rather than fact.

No blame

If something should go wrong within your department, it is important not to automatically assume that the person who is undertaking the task is at fault. It might be that there are inhibiting factors within the organization itself, poor cross-functional links, for example. It could be that your initial instructions were not as clear as they should have been, and you have not offered sufficient support during the project for that person to be able to undertake the task or responsibility appropriately.

Within your department good news needs to be accredited to an individual in the team. The group should share bad news, and everyone should trust you as a team leader/manager to look after them in a disaster. It is important to give credit where it is deserved (you get reflected credit), and shield your staff from disasters. People clearly have to learn from their mistakes but you need to take issue with that person behind closed doors. Part of this process is to constantly be creating expectations for your people to aspire to. In *Kaizen* there is no such thing as the status quo.

A recent report by the UK Government's Department of Trade and Industry found that many organizations claimed to have a no-blame environment until something went wrong and then everyone looked for somebody to blame! The way to ensure mediocrity is to put people at risk, blame them for their failings, and guess what, they won't expand and take risks for fear of failing. Bill Gates claims that he will not employ a senior manager unless he or she has made mistakes.

Making improvements constantly

Searching for new and different ways to undertake a task or activity is an essential element in the creation of *Kaizen*. The assumption is that everyone has two jobs: doing the job and improving the job. A new performance standard will be created through the improvement; however, this performance standard will only be in place for as long as it takes for another individual or team to find a better way of doing it.

This performance monitoring would appear to be the obvious approach to adopt, but as Imai has put it 'Yes, it is common sense, but not common practice!'

THE BIGGER PICTURE

Looking at the bigger picture, what else needs to be in place for *Kaizen* to succeed? It is vital that the organizational structure contains the least number of management levels, and forges the shortest possible chain of command. The structure needs to be an inverse triangle with all activities being focused towards the customer.

There should also be a member of the top team who is responsible for the implementation of the *Kaizen* programme, and a timed action plan needs to be in place. This action plan should address the following points.

- Who are to be the key personnel to champion and take forward the changes, and to allocate responsibility for their implementation? Even if the intention is for the teams to become self managed, ideally the team needs to select initially a team leader to act as a facilitator for the group.
- How all members of the organization will ultimately be involved in the process and the specific objectives they will be expected to achieve.
- The communication channels that should be in place company wide.
- The training and development required to support the changes.
- The dedication of sufficient resources to the change process to ensure success.

However well thought out, few plans can ever predict unexpected events and outcomes, be they created by internal activity or the external environment. This makes it essential to monitor the plan continually, and to consider changes where appropriate.

It is important to have a clear and consistent shared view of the future. Staff will often be critical of the company's mission statement being displayed in reception without the environment in any way reflecting the message in the statement. The visionary message needs to be communicated and part of the living everyday activity of the company.

Senior management commitment to Kaizen is vital for the sustained changes and the organizational culture needs to be developed and supported.

Senior management commitment to *Kaizen* is vital for the sustained changes and the organizational culture needs to be developed and supported.

Let us look in more depth at what this actually means. Simply put, culture is a set of generally accepted principles used to guide day-to-day activities in a subconscious way for members of an organization – it is 'the way we do things around here'. But cultural change is slow and difficult to make. Limited change can occur in one particular team without senior management but it is difficult to sustain these changes without the backing and support of senior management.

Culture evolves as a result of all the actions of the entire organization over time. Management support provides integration and consistency throughout the organization versus fractionalization by departments and units. Management is the final authority for time and money allocation, which will ultimately affect the culture through rewards, training programmes, recruiting new change agents and other such mechanisms.

✻ Management has a responsibility to align the informal organization (culture driven) and formal organization (management designed structure) to maximize efficiency and effectiveness. Culture must be mobilized to support a formal organization because without the support of the informal organization, the effectiveness of the formal organization will be diminished. Culture ultimately controls what, how, why, when and *if* things get done. ✻

As our client, Wade Wnuk, has said:

> *Management must stay the course and remain true to the change. They should not waver. Detractors must be openly confronted in a positive way. There must be a direct relentless effort to open up discussion of dissent.*

Culture change to introduce *Kaizen* is not a quick-fix programme, but a slow evolution towards desired behaviour, especially if high turnover is unacceptable as a method to introduce change agents. Should, however, certain personnel consistently inhibit the introduction of the new culture then they need to be supported by the appropriate methodology, be it through mentoring, training or some form of supportive development programme. If there should then be little or no change in their behaviour, they will need to be removed from the company. Scepticism can be rife during any change programme, and unless people can feel and see that changes are occurring, they will wait until the new initiative 'blows over', and in the meantime see how colleagues are siding up, and take a 'political allegiance'.

Honda Motors (UK) – A Continuous Improvement Case Study

To illustrate a radical approach that has been adopted to introduce continuous improvement, I would like to share with you the information I gathered from John Boylan who was Employee Development Manager during the changes that occurred within Honda Motors UK between 1994–6. John, at that time, worked in the Sales and Distribution side of the business, which up until 1993 had operated on a limited import quota basis. Demand had always far exceeded supply and so both this unit and the dealerships had effectively operated as order takers, and very profitable ones at that.

When the quota was lifted it was decided that the key to continued success was to introduce a programme which focused on continuous improvement and customer satisfaction.

The first step in the journey was to first determine the structure, then look at the jobs and skills required to make the structure effective. Then the whole process of evaluating their current staff began. Anyone applying for a new position, be they already in the company or an external candidate, had to go through a thorough examination of their capabilities. This included the use of case studies, role plays, psychometric testing and group exercises.

Inevitably many of the staff didn't like the approach and left, but those who were successful were quickly recognized as being more highly motivated than the previous occupants of the job.

In the first three years of the change process there were over 80 positional changes in a division of 120. Of the four senior managers only one was an internal hire. Line managers were moved into the field and field staff into line management. Without pursuing a fixed job rotation policy, many staff were moved into totally different areas to fulfil specific projects.

Every employee was reviewed, and assessed in the following categories: having potential; might have potential; those who would stand still; those requiring career counselling.

An analysis of employee skill gaps was then undertaken, and a modular training programme developed to encompass both the group and individual requirements. The training itself was undertaken by using internal resources or external consultants, and was done as and when required.

A graduate training programme was also established and development roles were identified for those staff who showed potential.

Regular department and divisional meetings were established to ensure that everyone knew what was happening, and had the opportunity to ask questions.

On the dealership side two programmes were launched to improve standards and refocus attention on customer care. Initially there was scepticism within the dealerships that this was just another fad. Honda Motors UK showed the seriousness of their intent by severing relationships with those dealerships that did not improve their customer care. Honda also sought feedback from the remaining dealerships as to how they could improve their service to them and, importantly, acted on this information. This process was then repeated throughout the year, and dealer advisory committees were established to work jointly with the main distribution unit to achieve the changes.

So, what has ultimately been achieved by these changes?

Between 1993 and 1996 sales went from 25,000 units to 45,000, and the J D Power survey named Honda as the overall number one manufacturer in the UK for 1996.

Customer focus

Underpinning continuous improvement is a long-term focus on customers' needs. A quality product and quality of service are inextricably bound into the manufacturing-selling chain. All organizations will claim that they adhere to the concept of 'quality'; it is your entry into the marketplace. What is now required is a need to be memorable through the added value service that you offer.

So how can you constantly instil the importance of the customer in your workforce?

Avon Cosmetics – A Customer Focus Case Study

Avon introduced the concept of continuous improvement using Philip Crosby's Quality and Improve (QPI) process. Groups of 12 were selected from different departments and from a cross-section of levels of responsibility. QPI leaders were selected and went through an extensive training programme in the USA. Those who were not based in the UK then returned to cascade down their training to other team leaders.

Classic measurement systems were introduced to monitor cost savings in production, and quality improvements. A vendor management programme was then introduced to advocate those who were selling the products and recognition and reward system put in place to reflect and encourage the changes. To improve and develop the concept of the internal customer, service levels were rated for each department, problem areas identified and action plans agreed. This acted as a firm foundation for Service Level Agreements to be introduced. A substantial budget was put in place to research and monitor the external customers' needs on an ongoing basis.

So what were the results?

In Years 1 and 2, sales growth was 33.6 per cent; profit growth was 256 per cent.

In Year 1 cost savings of £235,000 were achieved.

By Year 3 cost savings had risen to £3,300,000.

Every visual aid should be used to highlight your customer focus, be it via notice boards internally, on your corporate stationery, or by circulating customer success stories by e-mail. Everyone internally should be aware of your product range, and your positioning in the marketplace, not just your sales staff.

External research on at least an annual basis to clarify your customers' needs is a must, but also internal research is needed to identify poor internal customer care.

According to the *Harvard Business Review*, if you can reduce customer defections by just 5 per cent you can increase profitability by between 25 and 85 per cent. Your people should therefore not only be examining complaints, but also non-repeat business to ensure a continual reduction in the cause of complaints.

The exploration of every way to add value to the services that you offer should be a journey without an end, and the whole ethos of the organization should be geared to encourage this.

IMPLEMENTING KAIZEN

Having looked at the organizational structure, management's responsibilities and the need for customer focus, I am now going to move on to explore in very practical ways how to implement *Kaizen*.

There are three key elements that need to be considered: first systems and procedures need to be in place (e.g. BS5750/ISO9002). Second the technologies need to be in line with requirements, be these IT or telecoms based. Third your people need to be on board, and committed to change and development.

Figure 1.1   *The three key elements*

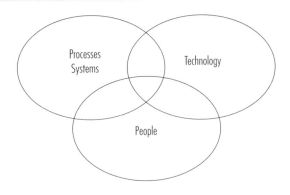

No part of this tripartite arrangement can work in isolation. You can have the greatest systems, procedures and technologies in place, but unless you have your people on board *Kaizen* cannot develop. Likewise, you can have your people on board, but if they do not have the appropriate technology, or systems and procedures in place to support them, they will not be able to be as effective as they would like.

One of the key concepts of *Kaizen* is the elimination of waste (*muda*). In a Japanese manufacturing environment where they have adopted the concept, they have what is known as the 'morning market' at the beginning of each shift. The purpose of this meeting is to examine the defects from the previous production run, and look for ways of improving the manufacturing process. In an administration function this will take the form of a weekly meeting to review all the suggestions for improvement that team members have made, which of these ideas can be put immediately into effect, and which ideas should be taken forward to a cross-functional meeting stage.

Measurement of waste is just as applicable in the service sector. During a training session that I ran in Singapore I met a group from Ascott International who had realized increases in income of 7 per cent, in employee productivity of 5.3 per cent, and in profitability of 6 per cent. These savings were achieved in a two year time span through the elimination of waste, which they told the group could only have happened as a result of a total cultural change to adopt the principles of *Kaizen*.

Ascott Singapore – A Kaizen Case Study

This organization offers top of the range serviced apartments and operates in a highly competitive, price sensitive environment in South East Asia.

Peter Tunge, Deputy Director, told me:

Our objective in adopting Kaizen was to balance growth, profit and excellence. Clearly, we could achieve growth by increasing our rates if the market was growing, or by identifying new markets. However, to achieve growth in the price sensitive recessive environment that we are operating in is another matter. Profit could possibly be improved by offering lower quality goods, but this would affect the third part of the equation, excellence. This could certainly affect our discerning existing and potential client base. They expect and demand excellence from the service that we offer them.

We decided to adopt Kaizen through recognition of the following values:

- *customer satisfaction in an ever-changing 'expectations' landscape*
- *employee-customer bonding*
- *open acknowledgement of problems and solutions*
- *relationship management between operating units and corporate office*
- *sharing information on performance and guests' particular needs and expectations*

- *empowerment for employees*
- *on the job and off the job training, with the syllabus being far more extensive than is usual, in order to cater comprehensively for the guests' needs. For example, learning about added value services such as pre-setting the TV set to enable tape recording of a guest's favourite programme, and educating all the staff to have fingertip knowledge of good local restaurants, places of interest, and how to get there. This information was gleaned during a '500 questions and answers' learning programme run on a regular basis for all members of staff.*

The measurements that were chosen were as follows:

- *income per square foot*
- *employee productivity*
- *cost efficiency*
- *profitability.*

Once we had released the creative input of our staff through the introduction of quality circles, ideas for improvement started to come on a regular basis. One of the more controversial ideas that we introduced paid off in a relatively short period of time. This was to offer a complimentary limousine service from the airport to the Ascott and Palm Court Apartments both in Singapore. We also offered check in within the comfort of the apartment rather than the reception area. We became the first service apartment operators to offer this service, and we started to gain market share as bookings picked up shortly after the service was introduced.

We believe that it is indeed a feat to do as we have done and achieve growth, profit and excellence. More often than not, growth and excellence are achieved at the expense of profit. Profit and growth may be had at the cost of excellence, or profit and excellence with little growth. It is due to Kaizen that we were melded into a team, and as a team we were able to introduce improvements in all these areas.

Teams

At the beginning of this chapter I talked about the need for people to have support. This can be aided by the grouping of personnel into teams to support individuals in their quest for problem solving or creativity. Team leaders need to be trained and developed themselves, so that they understand group dynamics, people management skills, and, importantly, how to bring out the creativity of team members.

Teams can take various forms. They can be natural teams, in other words, teams who would naturally meet in a department (e.g. Customer Service), or QIP (Quality Improvement) Teams, who would work on problem-solving projects to resolve a specific issue. There could also be QSO (Quality Strategic Objectives) Teams which could exist to ensure that the company attends to longer term issues of quality such as leadership, commitment, training, benchmarking and communication. The whole issue of team development is going to be explored in more depth by Bob Hersowitz in Chapter 6.

In the initial stages of introducing cultural change you will have certain individuals within the organization who will naturally rise to the challenge and become your 'internal champions'. As I have indicated earlier, there needs to be the support of mentoring, training and development for staff at all levels. However, as you lose personnel who are unable or unwilling to make the changes required, you will need to have a recruitment strategy in place which reflects your human resource (HR) strategy. Skill sets and competencies in particular areas are a given requirement, but attitude is also of importance. The characteristics of a *Kaizen* person are as follows:

- a forward-looking approach
- attention to detail
- receptive to constructive advice
- willingness to take responsibility
- pride in his or her work and organization
- a willingness to co-operate.

During the recruitment process these traits need to be borne in mind. As a *Kaizen* culture develops internally, increasingly the teams themselves become involved with the final selection of the person or people to join their team.

If you are looking toward creating a culture of expansion, you need to have in place people who are prepared to push the boundaries, and create new ideas for improvement. They may be in any part of the organization, not just in the new product development or the design department. Rosabeth Moss Kanter in her book *The Change Masters* calls them 'corporate entrepreneurs'.

She describes people's ability to become specialists in their functions so that they could enact changes and became excellent builders of systems. Others became expert at cutting losses. Some developed into ardent social pioneers and others became expert in reading shifts and trends in the marketplace. The key point Moss Kanter makes is that these corporate entrepreneurs contribute immeasurably to *improving* the existing business rather than creating new businesses.

And finally, to really capture the minds and spirits of your new people as they come on board, you need to have an induction process in place to create a positive way of thinking in your new members of staff. They need to gain a full picture of the organization itself, its goals and aspirations, and the culture and values that you have internally. They also need to feel that they are not just going to be a cog in a wheel, but will be offered development opportunities not only to advance within the company, but also to develop as an individual.

Sally Vanson at MCL in Tunbridge Wells has developed an excellent induction process, which is far more comprehensive than you usually find in UK organizations.

The MCL Group – An Induction Case Study

The MCL Group in Tunbridge Wells is an importer of Mazda cars. They have not only an excellent induction process, but also have a familiarization programme for all personnel which runs on a quarterly basis throughout the year.

Prior to a new employee actually joining the organization they have a 'buddy' assigned to them, who hierarchically comes from the same level as them, and has a similar lifestyle. They speak to each other on the telephone, and possibly meet prior to the person's first day at work. During the first weeks on the job, the 'buddy' is always available for any small practical issues that the new person might need to know about.

On Day 1 the 'buddy' meets the new person at 10.00 after all the rest of the staff are at work, and informally takes him or her for a coffee and shows them the layout of the building. They then go to meet the personnel department to go through practical details such as taking the P45 and salary payments and then at 12.30pm they meet their line manager who will take them informally to the pub for lunch. The afternoon is then spent in the department familiarizing themselves with the work throughput and meeting the rest of the team.

Each new employee is given a tailored induction programme with three or four meetings organized for each half-day during a two-week period. These meetings will be for secretaries, for example, to meet with other secretaries, managers with other managers. For the remaining part of each day during this period they will work in their own department with their team.

At the end of the two-week period there is a review with the HR Manager. During this session each new employee is given the opportunity to specify ongoing personal development requirements. This could vary from simple requests, such as learning a new software package, through to having the opportunity to visit dealerships, or a trip to Japan (which could last as long as six months).

At four weeks all employees go through a customer orientation programme, working on the basis that everyone in the company should be capable of promoting the product range, and it is obligatory that they should drive every model of Mazda car that is distributed by MCL. Great emphasis is also put on the concept of the internal customer.

Development then continues with 'on the job' training with their line manager, going through ISO procedures, etc. After four months Sally Vanson then meets with them again to agree work objectives for the rest of the year, and there is final agreement with the line manager. At this point their development needs to be reviewed again, and Sally makes sure that they have seen the business plan. Domestic arrangements are also reviewed if relocation has taken place.

At the end of four months all new employees are fully inducted and then move on to a regular performance review. The 360 degree appraisal system is now being introduced. To keep everyone fully informed of other department activities there is a three-day familiarization programme every quarter. All employees in the organization can attend, and can choose whether they wish to be on a one, two or three day programme. All the management team gives a presentation on Day 1, covering products, sales and strategic objectives. On Day 2 in the morning the Group Resources department talks about the role of human resource development, Personnel's objectives and the support the group can offer. In the afternoon there is a presentation on the future developments of Mazda. On Day 3 all employees are encouraged to visit other sites or dealerships, and even get to see the cars being off-loaded from the ships.

> Through the comprehensiveness of this development programme all employees are kept fully in touch with every aspect of the business and their skills and competencies are developed, measured and fine-tuned to complement this rapidly expanding and profitable organization.

USING KAIZEN AS A SPRINGBOARD

Several organizations have found that once they have adopted and adapted the fundamental principles of *Kaizen* they have needed to move on to a more focused and integrated approach and align quality improvements efforts around a common vision. *Hoshin kanri*, a planning, implementation and review system for managing change, has been used in this context. In essence the wording translates as policy management, and Japanese authors have stressed a consensual and directional essence in its meaning: 'a shining light from the metal of a compass needle to show the way forward'. Improvements are tied to, and focused around strategic priorities first and foremost, working on the premise of doing a handful of things well. An important influence on *hoshin kanri's* development in the West has been the successful implementation of the process within Hewlett-Packard. Other organizations in the West have adopted the practice but used a divergence of names such as 'Managing for Results' at the Xerox Corporation, 'Policy Deployment' in parts of AT&T, and 'Policy Management' at Florida Power and Light.

SUMMARY

Continuous improvement means, inevitably, a changing of attitudes, behaviour, work methodologies, the development of systems and procedures. It involves everyone and needs everyone's commitment. But at the end of the day it is a tremendous opportunity to change your working life for the better. The trouble with opportunity is that it often comes disguised as hard work. Continuous improvement is a ticket to the game rather than the game itself. So what is the game? It's about gaining and maintaining competitive advantage, driving fear out of your organization, helping everyone to contribute through training and development so that everyone feels needed, valued, and supported as an individual.

CHAPTER 2

How Kaizen Developed . . . and Developed . . . and Develops

CHRIS PATRICK

Director, Europe Japan Centre

THERE IS NOTHING MYSTERIOUS ABOUT the word *Kaizen*. It is a word used in everyday conversation in Japanese, simply meaning improvement. As a management concept, however, it was first used in the 1970s, with the meaning of a systematic approach to continuous improvement. Since then, as we will see, the concept has been expanded, transplanted and revitalized many times. It has grown from being essentially a quality initiative in Japan to being a part of everyday working life for many people around the globe. The fact that it has survived and prospered suggests that the concept is robust, and that it will continue to offer powerful support to organizations in many spheres of activity.

INTRODUCTION

The 'birth' of *Kaizen* as a management concept is closely bound up with Japan's recovery and growth after World War II, although many of its common-sense principles are much older and can frequently be found in organizations outside Japan. Within post-war Japan there was clearly a pressing need to make manufacturing industry efficient, so companies could provide much needed goods for the home market and also begin to penetrate export markets. This led some of the major manufacturers to look for ways to build on the strength of team structures in their companies and to harness the full contribution of all their employees. Quality circles, suggestion schemes, team meetings and many specific manufacturing techniques, including Just in Time and *Kanban* inventory control systems, became increasingly common.

By the 1970s, some companies had integrated these ideas into a more all-embracing philosophy, which covered organizational structures and management behaviour as well as quality initiatives and production techniques. Then, in 1986, Masaaki Imai published his influential book entitled *Kaizen: the Key to Japan's Competitive Success*, in which he showed how a number of companies were successfully using these ideas in an integrated way: *Kaizen*, as a management concept, had been born.

STAGE I: KAIZEN IN
MANUFACTURING IN JAPAN

At the heart of the *Kaizen* approach was the idea of small, but continuous, incremental improvements, originating mainly from the people who knew best about manufacturing: the people on the shopfloor who were doing it. Ideas should be encouraged and rewarded; good ideas should spread through the organization both vertically and horizontally via formal structures put in place to maximize communication.

At the heart of the Kaizen approach was the idea of small, but continuous, incremental improvements.

Employees should work towards specific goals: the elimination of wasted time, money, materials and effort (*muda* [waste in Japanese]), raising quality in products, services, relationships, etc and cutting costs. The Japanese system of life-time employment and strong company loyalty may have made some Japanese employees pre-disposed to support these goals, but in addition, management should consciously work to train and develop their employees, share rewards with them and generally support their efforts in every way possible.

The story of Japanese industry during the 1960s, 1970s and early 1980s has many such cases. Academic research has also shown, many times, that the phenomenal growth rates recorded by much of Japanese industry during this period were in no small measure attributable to these *Kaizen* elements, although many other factors, including government support and pricing policy, were also influential.

It is important to note that at this stage, the adoption of *Kaizen* was largely limited to manufacturing companies. Automotive companies, such as Toyota, were among the pioneers, but most other large manufacturers quickly followed suit, introducing the systems and attitudes in their own companies, then in their suppliers' companies, and more recently even in their suppliers' suppliers' companies.

STAGE II: EXPORTING KAIZEN

When Japanese companies began to set up factories in the USA and Europe in the 1970s, they generally brought *Kaizen* with them. Teamworking, *Kaizen* problem-solving groups and suggestion schemes

---

SMED

A well-known example is SMED (Single Minute Exchange of Dies), an improvement which Shingeo Shingo and his team at Toyota introduced in 1970. After hearing that a Volkswagen factory in Germany could change dies on its presses in two hours, whereas it took Toyota four hours, the Japanese team worked to reduce this time to under two hours. After successfully achieving this goal, however, the team continued to seek further improvement, so that it was soon significantly quicker than the German factory.

---

became a common feature of Japanese companies in the West, usually, although by no means always, meeting with acceptance from local workforces. Research by Oliver and Wilkinson[1] indicates the high proportion of Japanese companies in the UK which had introduced key elements of *Kaizen* by 1991:

Practice	In use, planned or being implemented (%)
Team briefings	92
In-company [direct] communications	83

Typically, *Kaizen* practices were seen to increase productivity. Again according to Oliver and Wilkinson,[2] at 'K-Electric', a major Japanese corporation in the UK, for example, between 1987 and 1990, improvements included:

- a 35 per cent reduction of work-in-progress
- reduction of standard times by 15 per cent
- saving of 11 per cent of floor space.

The export of *Kaizen* was not completely problem-free, however. Trades unions tended to object on the grounds that workers were expected to work harder, often for the same money, that differentials were eroded or eliminated by the flexible work patterns demanded, and that in several cases Japanese management would agree only to single-union recognition. For individual employees the main point of difficulty was often the pressurized pace of work. While some people appreciated

A London Noodle Restaurant

A chain of Japanese noodle restaurants in London, opened its first branch in 1992. It currently has three branches in London, and plans to open more branches shortly not only in the UK but also in the USA and Europe. The restaurants offer a high-speed, high-tech. dining experience. At the heart of this success is *Kaizen*. The philosophy underlies the whole management of the company, and ensures that the logistics of turning the tables ten or more times per day works smoothly and efficiently. Turnover is already in excess of £3 million a year, and industry sources believe the company may be planning a flotation in 1999.

The Canterbury Crusaders

In New Zealand the revival of the 'Canterbury Crusaders', a professional rugby team, has been attributed by their sports psychologist to a style based on *Kaizen*. When the team won the national championship in 1998 *Kaizen* received a big boost both in New Zealand and in rugby circles worldwide.

the benefits and attitudes of teamworking, others found the atmosphere of factories such as Nissan oppressive and exploitative.

Western companies, observing the economic success of Japanese factories in the West, were not slow to try and adopt some of the principles of Japanese working. Unipart, the Rover Group and Lucas Industries were among the first large companies in the UK to follow this route; many smaller companies, including suppliers to Japanese companies who were sometimes trained by the Japanese companies, also looked to *Kaizen*.

The early success of some manufacturing companies in adopting *Kaizen* led relatively quickly in the West to the introduction of *Kaizen* in non-manufacturing environments. Service companies, government agencies and even sports teams began to see how they could adopt *Kaizen* principles, and many succeeded.

STAGE III: ADDING WESTERN FLAVOURS

In most cases, Western management sought to take some of the Japanese elements out of *Kaizen*, often starting with the very word *Kaizen*. Sometimes the English translation, continuous improvement, was simply used instead; in other cases completely different expressions have been used: Boeing's *Kaizen* workshops, for example, are known as Accelerated Improvement Workshops. As a result, many people outside Japan are involved in *Kaizen* practices without knowing that they are.

More fundamentally, Western companies adopting *Kaizen* have had to come to terms with a number of issues which differ from the situation in Japan. This has meant devising new ways of effecting the necessary shifts both in culture and in management:

From a Western model. . .	to a Kaizen model
• Individual working	Teamworking
• Unitary leadership	Delegation, participation, consensus
• Making do	Continuous improvement
• Rigidity and specialism	Flexibility and collaboration
• One-way communication	Two-way communication

Some Western problem areas

Kaizen has typically needed to focus efforts more strongly in the West than in Japan in the following areas.

Re-definition of the role and style of managers. Traditionally in large companies in Japan, senior managers often play a largely rubber-stamping role. They are involved in setting the overall vision, but then tend to delegate decision making to groups. Consensus, participation and involvement are important concepts in oiling the wheels of the organization. Typically senior managers have held posts in many different departments within the company, and have a broad understanding of the whole organization, although their knowledge in any one area is frequently lower than their more specialized counterparts in Western organizations. This again tends to mean it makes sense to leave decisions to groups and to people, frequently middle managers, lower down the organizational hierarchy. All of these factors fit well with the *Kaizen* principles of participation and teamworking.

For Western companies which have adopted *Kaizen*, the role of managers has often been a particularly difficult area. In many early cases, managers thought it would be enough to introduce *Kaizen* on the shopfloor, and that their own role would not need to change. This proved not to be the case.

Managers in the West of course need to preserve their individuality – nobody has talked about turning Japanese – but certain attributes, which are not necessarily the preserve of the East anyway, have been found to be extremely helpful in creating the sort of organizing where *Kaizen* flourishes. In companies where *Kaizen* has been successfully introduced in the West, leaders have tended to be:

- open-minded
- able to conceptualize
- willing to learn new behaviours
- team-orientated
- flexible and adaptable
- first-class communicators
- able to listen and respond.

One lesson that has emerged very clearly in the West during this process is that these attributes do not have to come naturally; they can be learnt. Innovative methods of fostering this development have also emerged, as the United Technologies case study on page 32 illustrates.

Changing attitudes in the workforce. It has often been said that Japanese, or Asian, workforces are more naturally inclined to *Kaizen* than Western workforces: in general, people work harmoniously in teams, are willing to put the good of the organization ahead of their own interests, give 110 per cent effort and work hard to avoid conflict. While this is clearly an exaggerated picture, it is certainly true that, until recently when the picture is beginning to change, Japanese companies have been able to rely on the dedication of their workforces to a far greater extent than Western companies, and that this has proved a very fertile backdrop for *Kaizen*.

In general, organizations have spent more time convincing Western workforces of the benefits of *Kaizen* than convincing managers. In practice, however, it has proved less problematic than changing the attitudes of managers. Many workforces in Europe and the USA have welcomed aspects of *Kaizen*, in particular the opportunity to have ideas listened to, to do a better job with less re-working or waste, and to participate more fully in the organization. Problems have arisen when:

- additional effort or improved results are not rewarded
- more and more is expected, resulting in stress
- management is not seen to be supporting *Kaizen* principles.

Some Western solutions

In an effort to make *Kaizen* work well in their organizations, Western managers and workforces have coped with these various difficulties in different ways.

Training All companies which commit themselves to *Kaizen* know that extensive training is necessary, not only in specific problem-solving skills but at least as importantly in 'softer' aspects such as teamworking, team leadership, working attitudes, etc. It is generally thought that *Kaizen* in the West takes at least five years to be properly embedded in the company culture. For large Western organizations this means that it has been worth considering establishing their own training institute or 'university'. Unipart, the British car part manufacturer, was a fore-runner in the UK, when it opened its in-house university, Unipart U. At Polygram, the London-based entertainment company, managers set up their own programme, running seminars for each other, rather than booking external courses. In the USA, General Electric, Xerox and Motorola are all firmly committed to their own university-style programmes.

Stress-relief Of course stress is not associated only with organizations which have adopted *Kaizen*. Many of the stress-inducing factors are common to most organizations and walks of life. Organizations which listen to their people and are committed to responding to their concerns have increasingly needed to be seen to take action to relieve stress. At the Nissan factory in Sunderland, where there have been many complaints of stress, a number of measures have been taken both to deal with the causes and to relieve the symptoms. These include the recruitment of a company physiotherapist. Other companies have tried to develop more family-friendly policies, including workplace nurseries, flexible work times, etc., to help employees balance home and working lives less stressfully.

Other companies which have adopted *Kaizen* claim that *Kaizen* practices tend rather to reduce stress. According to Compac Print in the UK, up-skilling and re-skilling are very positive directions.

United Technologies

In 1998 United Technologies, owners of businesses including Otis lifts, Sikorsky helicopters and engine suppliers Pratt and Whitney, established a training institute to teach its own staff and its suppliers new production and management techniques to cut costs and improve quality. The company thinks that many of the major management ideas of recent years, including specifically *Kaizen*, have only reached large companies and that small companies, including their own suppliers, are still lagging behind. The institute is known as Ito University, after Yuzuru Ito, a Japanese manufacturing consultant who works with United. Training will be given not only in the USA, but also in Europe and Asia.

A further *Kaizen*-based innovation of the institute is that the trainers will be United's own factory workers, who will teach not only their peers but also higher-ranking executives about techniques and practices on the shopfloor.

The best means to counter stress is the ability to go home at night knowing you've done a good job. If you can build that philosophy into your people, so that they get a kick out of upgrading their performance, you're on the right track. Stress is just a negative way of perceiving pressure, and that can be a positive thing.

Motivation and rewards Strong feelings of company loyalty and dedication in Japan mean that less emphasis was traditionally placed on motivation. Within *Kaizen*, suggestions have generally been rewarded with token amounts of money, depending on the success of the suggestion. Outside Japan, however, it has mostly proved necessary for the organization to provide more positive and more regular motivation in order to keep the momentum going. Some organizations have opted for financial incentives such as one-off awards, share options, profit sharing, etc. Some have put more stress on celebrating success. At Honda, executives flew to a plant in Mexico to hear for themselves the success of a problem-solving team and to congratulate the team personally.[3]

STAGE IV: KAIZEN IN
TIMES OF TROUBLE

By the early 1990s, *Kaizen* had become very well established in the West. A survey conducted by the Europe Japan Centre in 1993 showed that 94 per cent of senior managers in large UK companies were aware of *Kaizen* and that 88 per cent of senior managers in large manufacturing companies had actual experience of *Kaizen*. The word *Kaizen* has even appeared in the Oxford English Dictionary.

Troubles in the East

Ironically, the success of *Kaizen* in the West corresponded with the bursting of the economic bubble in Japan and with growing doubts in Japanese companies about the ability of their management techniques to cope with the new economic problems. Could gradual, if continuous, improvement still have a role to play in a world where more radical change suddenly seemed called for? When a Toyota spokesperson proclaimed '*Kaizen* is not enough', fundamental questions began to be asked.

In Japan it is currently too soon to say how or whether organizations will manage to answer these questions successfully and reverse the poor results which many are experiencing in the wake of low domestic consumption, downturns in the Asian markets, lower competitiveness of Japanese products in the West and many other factors. There is much discussion of changes in human resources policies and organizational structures, but few companies have as yet taken truly radical action, with most sticking to *Kaizen* principles and the system of promotion and remuneration by seniority.

In the early 1990s, Japanese organizations identified a number of factors which they considered vital for future growth but where employees were typically weak. These included:

- risk-taking
- entrepreneurial attitudes
- keenness to undertake change.

Innovation and Kaizen

A refiner of precious metals has its head office in London but operates in 38 countries. In many respects, the company has tried to take the best from a number of systems and from them to create its own corporate culture.

Although the company is global, individuals are easily 'noticed', according to management. The company is decentralized and operates via four divisions. Communication is open and company wide and there is a strong team spirit. Innovation and *Kaizen* are both part of the corporate culture.

When they join the company, graduates are generally placed in customer-service teams, where they are 'given the opportunity to shine'. Action-oriented people are particularly prized. For bright people, there are many opportunities to travel and to move to other parts of the business.

Considerable emphasis is placed on training: an intensive series of two-day modules for graduate recruits is followed by on-the-job training. Fast-track middle managers can join a management development programme, and senior managers may attend courses at INSEAD or Harvard.

According to the Corporate Research Foundation, the company today is characterized by fast decision making and local responsibility, together with a reputation for integrity.

The company of today is much less bureaucratic, and a lot slicker and faster.

Answers in the West?

Interestingly, these are all factors where the West is perceived to be stronger than Japan. Not surprisingly, therefore, it was companies such as Honda and Sony, which are strongly international companies, which were at the forefront of moves in this area. To try and foster these qualities, several companies, including, for example, parts of Honda, introduced the idea of rewarding and promoting employees according to their ability rather than according to seniority, as had been the case in the past. More recently, however, there is a growing feeling that this change in itself is not enough, and that to further stimulate creativity, risk-taking and entrepreneurship, more radical ideas need to be introduced, including new reward and promotion systems.

World Class Practices

A US manufactuer has adopted what it calls its World Class Practices programme. It is an internal programme that takes many elements from the Toyota Production System, which uses *Kanban* Production Systems, and other Japanese and non-Japanese techniques, and which also uses *Kaizen* events as a way to redesign the way work is done in the company.

The company is trying to follow World Class Practices not only in their manufacturing plants, but also in their offices, and among their suppliers. According to their CEO in July 1998:

> *Although we have only been at this for a couple of years and there is much, much more to be done, we have already seen very dramatic improvements in quite a lot of our operations.*

Between 1996 and 1998 working capital as a percentage of sales declined by 11 per cent to 15.2 per cent, and both quality and productivity improved dramatically.

Are innovation and *Kaizen* compatible? Can major changes of direction be undertaken by *Kaizen*-based organizations? Although some *Kaizen* experts think that Western managers still put too much emphasis on 'big bang' change, to the detriment of the *Kaizen* approach,[4] actual experience on the ground in the West seems to indicate that a *Kaizen* approach can and frequently does work successfully hand-in-hand with innovation. *Kaizen* by itself is not enough, but it does not have to exist in isolation.

The refiner of metals mentioned earlier is far from alone in taking this type of approach. Many organizations are amalgamating different management practices and finding that they can work together. *Kaizen* and *Kanban* (the two Ks) have long been used together. Other elements are increasingly being added to produce ways of operating which suit a particular organization at a specific time.

KAIZEN FOR THE FUTURE?

In many ways, *Kaizen* fits very well with the current and likely future concerns of major organizations worldwide:

- developing global strategies
- pursuing environmentally sound policies
- developing people and creativity
- adding shareholder value
- fostering innovation and risk-taking.

Developing global strategies

Kaizen has now proved that it can work in developed and emerging markets.

Many Japanese automotive and electronics companies have found that *Kaizen* has transplanted without difficulty to their factories in Malaysia, South Korea and Taiwan, and that the combination of lower production costs and effective *Kaizen* practices resulted in making these plants far more competitive than those in Japan.

At Honda factories around the world people refer to the three As, a shorthand for the three actuals (actual spot [*gemba*], the actual part [*gembutsu*] and the actual situation [*genjitsu*]); it is a kind of corporate language that people in the company take for granted.

Non-Japanese companies in Asia and South America, particularly affiliates and subsidiaries of US or European companies, have also been attracted by *Kaizen* and there are many examples of successful implementation, including for example Lucas and Singhal Bosch in India, and Ford in South America. Organizations such as the Japanese Association for Overseas Technical Scholarships (AOTS) are also spreading the *Kaizen* message in Africa, with particular success in Zambia.

Companies such as Toyota have long used essentially common *Kaizen* techniques in all their factories worldwide, leading to the benefits of standardization, a common corporate language and values and clear common goals.

For Japanese companies, common cultures of the sort being built up by Honda and Toyota offer many possibilities in terms of developing more creative global strategies, using fully the management talents not only of Japanese staff but of senior managers around the world. So far, with a few exceptions such as Sony, Japanese companies have been slow to realize this potential. Many non-Japanese companies are already making use of this type of common culture, but there remain many possibilities for greater use in the future.

Pursuing environmentally sound policies

A fundamental tenet of Kaizen is the elimination of waste [muda]. This is usually one of the clearest and quickest results of the introduction of Kaizen.

A fundamental tenet of *Kaizen* is the elimination of waste [*muda*]. This is usually one of the clearest and quickest results of the introduction of *Kaizen*. More broadly, the whole thrust of *Kaizen* is to make continuous improvements that make all processes more efficient and thereby more environmentally friendly; as a result, energy saving is frequently a continual benefit of *Kaizen*.

At Philips Electronics, for example, a company-wide initiative, Eco-Vision, was launched in mid-1998 with tough waste and energy improvement targets. In addition to targets of 35 per cent waste reduction, 25 per cent less water use and significantly reduced emissions, an increasing percentage of products will need to be 'eco-designed' by the year 2001, with all business lines producing flagship green products within 1998.

Kaizen's original 'Five Ss' of good housekeeping[5] have long been translated into an English equivalent and have become a natural part of life in many organizations. In organizations which have operated *Kaizen* for some time, it is no longer necessary for specific sessions to be timetabled in on these subjects: employees naturally follow these principles, with positive environmental results.

Developing people and creativity

Organizations which get the most from Kaizen are those which train and develop their people continuously.

A fundamental part of *Kaizen* is that it seeks to use the whole brain of everyone in the company. Organizations which get the most from *Kaizen* are those which train and develop their people continuously. Particularly in the West, training is increasingly focusing on creativity, not just for managers or leaders but for the whole workforce. The kind of new thinking described in later chapters in this book fits very well with the concept of *Kaizen*. Once people are 'hooked' on learning and improvement, it becomes a natural part of life, which can be built on and expanded. Whole-brain learning, accelerated learning and many other non-Japanese techniques can be employed to enhance the basic *Kaizen* skills.

Adding shareholder value

As companies become increasingly conscious of the need to meet shareholder, as well as customer and employee, expectations, they are seeking to add value to every part of their business. While this may involve 'big leaps' in terms of mergers, take-overs and other major structural changes, the everyday improvements in productivity and use of capital, as well as the increase in operational knowledge among employees, all of which come from *Kaizen*, are an important factor in adding value to the company. Particularly at times of economic trouble, *Kaizen* can help cut costs and increase efficiency, as the rapidly growing interest in *Kaizen* in Germany in the mid-1980s attests.

Fostering innovation and risk-taking

Although originally *Kaizen* was viewed as in some senses the opposite of innovation and risk-taking, the development of pools of flexible, well-informed and creative employees and leaders with the new leadership skills necessary for *Kaizen* has had the result of making organizations far better equipped in terms of their people for tackling innovation. *Kaizen* organizations can also have structures which allow them to make decisions which are based on close communication with customers and with other departments in the organizations, and then to move quickly.

SUMMARY

As we have seen, *Kaizen* is increasingly becoming a normal part of organizational life. *Kaizen* attitudes both in manufacturing and in service organizations are in many cases naturally assumed; it is the 'concrete heads', those who still resist change, rather than the *Kaizen*-orientated

Kaizen has moved from being a process-orientated approach to manufacturing to being a far broader base for business, or even general educational, development.

people who stick out as the exceptions. *Kaizen* has moved from being a process-orientated approach to manufacturing to being a far broader base for business, or even general educational,[6] development. We can sum up the main developments as follows.

It is even possible to detect signs of the emergence of virtual *Kaizen*: as working practices change, as new technology advances, some of the traditional, visible forms of *Kaizen* are disappearing.

Some of the Japanese companies which have used *Kaizen* practices for many years, for example, are finding that they no longer need to have improvement activities as such. In the past Nissan plants in Japan, for example, had frequent two-day improvement events, where problems were worked on intensively by shopfloor teams. In the last few years these activities have become rare. According to Nissan, this is:

> *because they have worked so well. The improvement concepts embodied in the two-day event have become an integral part of the workplace at Nissan.*[7]

Kaizen remains as an underpinning and inspiring principle. It provides the skills and attitudes for organizations to move successfully into the future. In doing so, organizations can be free to develop new structures, new types of teams, new styles of leaders. They may be able

Kaizen was:	Kaizen is:
used in manufacturing and focused on processes	used in all areas and focuses on people and their creativity, as much as on processes
originally a means of increasing efficiency and productivity	a broader set of values for business success throughout an organization
systematic processes and structures throughout an organization	a more flexible approach, frequently used in conjunction with other systems and ideas
attitudes and processes to be learnt	increasingly a natural way of organizational life, to be built on creatively in new business environments
based essentially around vertical and horizontal teams in the workplace	increasingly developing through new forms of teams (self-managed, leaderless, virtual, etc.) and structures

to combine innovation with continuous improvement, making leaps and then making improvements quickly and flexibly in the new situation. The training and attitudes which are an integral part of *Kaizen* should ensure organizations have the right kind of creative people to make these developments successful.

Notes

1. See *The Japanization of British Industry*, Nick Oliver and Barry Wilkinson, Blackwell Business, 1992

2. Op. cit., p. 233

3. For the full story, see *Powered by Honda: Developing Excellence in the Global Enterprise*, Dave Nelson, Rick Mayo and Patricia E. Moody, John Wiley & Sons Inc., 1998

4. See for example *Gemba Kaizen: The Common-Sense Approach to Business Management*, Masaaki Imai, McGraw-Hill, 1997

5. Seiri (sort) – clear out unnecessary things and eliminate them; Seiton (straighten) – make materials readily accessible; Seiso (scrub) – make sure environment is completely clean; Seiketsu (systematize) – clean regularly; Shitsuke (standardize) – do all these processes regularly and improve them continuously

6. Even in the sphere of education, Kaizen is gaining ground. Speaking in Kuala Lumpur in early 1998, Dr Ng Yan Goh, International Director of the Global Institute for Strategic Economic Development, stressed the need to instil Kaizen in schools in Malaysia, in order to 'develop new generation workers to be creative and inovative'

7. *Industry Week*, 1 September 1997

CHAPTER 3

Kaizen and the Team:
the Great Symbiosis

Introduction

———

The Principles of *Kaizen* and Organizational Culture

———

Kaizen and Organizational Strategy

———

Why Teams?

———

Preconditions and Characteristics of
High Performing Teams

———

Summary

MICHAEL COLENSO

Associate, Europe Japan Centre

THIS CHAPTER EXPLORES THE WAY in which *Kaizen* affects the culture of the organization and the way teams operate as the instruments of the organization's strategic intent. It explores the ten principles of *Kaizen* and their fit with the accepted criteria of good team performance. It shows how a *Kaizen* culture can be used to illuminate and help structure a team's purpose and the processes the team uses.

INTRODUCTION

The essence of a successful team is that it achieves synergy. That is it produces, as a collective and collaborative effort, better results than its members would be capable of if they were acting individually.

Kaizen cannot and does not claim to have invented the idea of harnessing the advantages of teaming in the workplace. The use of teams and teaming in an organizational environment attracted serious research first in the 1940s. A number of social psychologists observed successful teams at work in an attempt to develop a model which could be used to accelerate team development. This early research favoured the concept of the role of different kinds of individuals in teams. Benne and Sheets and others in the USA and Belbin in the UK isolated varieties of behaviour which, when they were exhibited by team members, tended to hasten a team's coming together and to improve the quality of its decision making.

Research by the Tavistock Institute in London developed a system called Socio-technical Design. It involved giving a team shared responsibility for the outcomes of its performance, and it was developed initially in the coal mining industry. Unsurprisingly the results generated better *per capita* output combined with a greater sense of job satisfaction among team members.

As Chris Patrick has pointed out in the last chapter, the immediate post-war Japanese industrial economy required an accelerated industrial output to meet hungry markets. Initially Japanese industry was characterized by relatively high production of low quality, cloned or derivative products. Confronted as Japan was with a lack of raw materials, a poor industrial infrastructure and no world class manufacturing capability, new means had to be found to access international markets. It was probably the quality circle concept which changed the game.

The quality circle involved creating a team of people from *gemba* (the place where it happened, the proverbial coalface) and tasking them to produce continuous improvement in the products and services they provided others, to improve the processes by which they did this, and to achieve higher customer satisfaction as a result. Thus *Kaizen* was born.

The competitive advantage of this team-based organization, coupled with *Kaizen* tasking, took a while to demonstrate its effectiveness. When it did so however, in the early 1960s, the results were spectacular. That great bastion of Western industry, the US auto industry, and the mighty inner keep of that industry, General Motors, the largest, most powerful and most profitable company in the history of time, started to lose market share to Japanese imports.

Epic competitive battles have raged ever since with the US auto manufacturers regaining, losing and regaining market share against Japanese imports. At the time of writing though, the Toyota plant in Kentucky which produces the US version of the Camry has the lowest build cost of any car in its class. The Camry has also achieved the largest US market share in its class. The Toyota factory is organized entirely on a team basis and built around the concept of *Kaizen*.

The effect of Kaizen on world business has been profound. It has provided new and higher criteria of quality, new standards for organizational efficiency, and above all it has worked to the profound advantage of the customer.

While the roots of *Kaizen* are over forty years old now, its principles, processes and values are highly appropriate to the modern organization. It can be, and is, argued that the collapse of the Japanese economy witnessed in the 1990s is a poor recommendation for *Kaizen*, but that lamentable event has more to do with the problems of crony capitalism than it has to do with *Kaizen*.

On the contrary, the effect of *Kaizen* on world business has been profound. It has provided new and higher criteria of quality, new standards for organizational efficiency, and above all it has worked to the profound advantage of the customer.

THE PRINCIPLES OF KAIZEN AND ORGANIZATIONAL CULTURE

Designed as a means to encourage continuous improvement, *Kaizen* has arguably been most successful in the West when it has become the basis of organizational culture.

Organizational culture is best defined as the belief systems which operate within the organization. Formed by acute observation of the way in which members of the organization behave, most employees have a consistent and shared idea of what is rewarded around here, what gets tolerated, what gets punished, what sort of behaviour receives attention, and what is ignored. Employees generally know how the organization approaches problem solving, how it enacts changes, and they can predict how it will react to events and circumstances both internal and external. These shared views constitute organizational culture.

Organizational culture is formed less by what the organization says than by what it does.

Organizational culture is formed less by what the organization says than by what it does. In those cases where what it says and what it does differ, employees are likely to become cynical and will regulate their behaviour to reflect practice rather than pronouncement. This in turn reinforces an organizational culture in which cynicism is legitimated by example.

Devising an organizational culture is a bit like inventing a religion, and I have never encountered an organization which approached organizational change with culture as the starting point. Rather culture is the means of supporting and helping deliver the organization's strategic intent. Put another way, in the right culture, employees behave in a way which favours those things which the organization has identified as the basis of its differentiation from its competitors, its plan for survival in a competitive world.

Kaizen's success is that it has frequently provided for Western companies not only a ready-made culture capable of supporting strategic intent, but also a number of highly relevant processes which go beyond the idea of enablement and actually provide the means of achieving elements of the strategy.

The congruence of *Kaizen* with modern organizational needs is compelling. To see just how relevant let us look at the ten main principles of *Kaizen* (see page 46).

These principles have all the hallmarks of the enlightened modern organization operating in a hypercompetitive, global, customer-dominated, cusp-of-the-millennium environment. If we add to this the ingredient of a sophisticated 'generation x' employee, one seeking personal development, empowerment, involvement and responsibility, *Kaizen* provides a convincing fit with contemporary organizational need.

Importantly these principles provide the basis of an organizational culture which is directly supportive of the strategic intent of many, if not most, organizations.

Kaizen sometimes overwhelms with the breadth and depth of the philosophy it offers. Often organizations pursue initiatives which are parts of *Kaizen*. Total Quality Management (TQM) is probably the

---

The Ten Main Principles of Kaizen

1. Focus on customers (external and internal).
2. Seek continuous improvement in products, services and processes.
3. Acknowledge and bring problems to the surface ('surface' problems).
4. Foster an environment of openness, honesty and frankness.
5. Use teams as the primary unit of organization.
6. Manage projects cross functionally.
7. Nurture supportive relationships, vertically in the organization as well as laterally.
8. Develop self discipline, a sense of personal responsibility and accountability.
9. Inform every employee – communicate unceasingly, communicate comprehensively, communicate in depth.
10. Set up employees for success, enable their achievement.

---

most common Western name for the core *Kaizen* concept of incremental improvement. More recently Business Process Re-engineering (BPR), as developed and championed by Michael Hammer, has generated a great deal of corporate use. Imaei, the most famous living proponent of *Kaizen* would describe BPR as eliminating *muda* – the elimination of waste, the excision of all activities which do not add value to the product or service. The concept of employee empowerment and the devolution of decision making to the point closest to the process equates approximately with *Kaizen*'s thinking about *gemba*.

KAIZEN AND ORGANIZATIONAL STRATEGY

Strategy or strategic intent is the means by which the organization plans to survive and prosper long term. It is a mistake to generalize about the strategy of all or even most organizations, but there are a

Strategy or strategic intent is the means by which the organization plans to survive and prosper long term.

number of common threads running through the strategic intent of most organizations. These commonalities occur because of the nature of the modern competitive environment, characterized as it is by the increasing dominance of the customer on the one hand, and the unpredictability of the markets on the other.

Most organizations are looking for:

- the enhancement of quality – to satisfy an ever more demanding customer;
- reduction of cost – to respond to increasingly intense global competition;
- ways of developing their employees so that the organization can:
  - achieve competitive advantage and differentiation by the way their employees interact with their clients
  - gain access to employees' innovative ability
  - enhance its skill base, its intellectual capital, if you prefer that phrase.

It is fair to say that any organization seeking to be world class will be managing itself to achieve these things. Since almost all organizations find themselves competing in a global economy anyway, economic survival depends on getting good at these things. Plainly a *Kaizen* culture in which the ten principles outlined above are enshrined and affecting the way people behave will help.

Just how does it work? What is the mechanism by which the behaviour of employees supports the organization's strategy? It starts with the need for employees to be clear about what the organization is trying to achieve. This may seem a mindless truism, but in many organizations developing the strategy is so far removed from the workforce that the communication gap is never adequately bridged. One of the ways around this is to involve employees in strategy development and I will return to this subject in Chapter 10.

Informed employees however, knowing and understanding what the company is trying to do to differentiate itself and to survive, have a clear sense of overall direction. If we then add to this a culture in which what gets rewarded, what punished, etc. is consistent with known overall direction then your people will:

- invest their discretionary effort in the areas which are believed to matter
- prioritize their responsibilities to conform to the organization's strategic intent

- make decisions based on the longer term criteria of the strategy rather than shorter term expediency
- measure and judge their performance and that of their staff using the criteria of the strategy.

What we are starting to see then is the culture and the strategy synchronized so that everybody is pulling in a common direction. It is obvious that *Kaizen* can, and for many organizations, does provide the cultural norms which achieve this synchronicity.

WHY TEAMS?

At the start of this chapter I suggested that teams delivered value only when they achieved synergy. What does synergy look like for an organization? What are the essential advantages which they offer?

- Improved productivity – successful teams develop the ability to accomplish more, faster.
- Improved creativity – cross functionality, or even the application of a number of different minds to the task usually produces original, 'out-of-the-box' thinking.
- Focus – properly tasked teams can solve intractable organizational problems.
- Development – serving on a team, participating in team activity provides good developmental experience, sometimes fast-track, for team members.
- Employee satisfaction – successful teams often have a good time, members also have a sense of achievement.

Traditionally, most organizations are built on the basis of functional activity. This involves locating specialist expertise in a series of discrete operating units. The organization's work then flows through each of the operating units where value is added by the application of the functional speciality of the unit.

This system has both advantages and disadvantages. On the positive side, great expertise can be developed in the functional units, the organization's resources can be accurately targeted, multiple developmental possibilities exist for staff, etc. On the negative side, the operating unit can lose sight of its customer in pursuit of the punctilious application of its expertise. The system can become cumbersome and slow down the workflows.

One of the ways in which these disadvantages can be overcome is by the introduction of cross-functional teams. This usually looks like a team tasked with a specific purpose, its members representing each of the functional capabilities resident in the operating units. *Kaizen* strongly advocates cross functionality and unifies the disparate intention of participants who serve on such teams by focusing on the customer and the pursuit of a well articulated purpose.

Putting a team together is a time-consuming, often lengthy process, requiring managerial time, usually (see Chapter 5) some strife and realignment, and above all, changed behaviour on the part of everyone associated with it.

What absolutely does not work is to announce, say, that the Accounts Department is now a team and do nothing to provide the developmental track necessary for the team to form, for the synergy to be generated, for the potential to be unlocked. Most organizations are littered with 'teams' which are not achieving synergy, with wary groups of participants who are not contributing their full potential.

It becomes important to be sparing in the use of the word 'team'. Do not call those who attend an information briefing a team, they are not, they are merely updating their information. The essential precondition for a team is that it knows and understands what it is there to achieve (purpose), and it knows how its achievements will be measured (objectives).

PRECONDITIONS AND CHARACTERISTICS OF HIGH PERFORMING TEAMS

Reviewing the extensive body of research into successful teams, a number of conditions and characteristics emerge which are present in high performing teams and absent in groups of people either mistakenly called teams or masquerading as such. You may find, as I have, that it is useful to think of two categories of criteria which successful teams must have in place. I describe these respectively as the Preconditions and the Characteristics.

Preconditions must be provided by those outside the team, usually those who set the team up and those to whom it reports. Preconditions have mostly to do with the operating environment of the team; its mandate, the clarity with which it understands its purpose and the way it is supported.

Characteristics on the other hand describe those things which teams can do on their own behalf to make themselves successful. Getting these characteristics right implies that members choose to conduct themselves in certain ways, regulate their behaviour and live up to the expectations of their fellow team members.

To help teams understand their roles and accelerate their development it helps if they have a knowledge of how teams work and the training to teach them about how to get better at being a team.

Preconditions

Purpose Successful teams have a clear sense of **why** they exist. That usually means they understand the strategic significance of why they have been set up. They see their role in the broader strategic plan, they understand how their success will contribute to the organization's strategic intent.

Empowerment Successful teams have a strong sense of being in charge of their own destiny. They believe themselves to be accountable for what they do, that they 'carry the can', and that they are responsible for their conduct. Their recommendations must be taken seriously by those to whom they report; their successes celebrated, their failures brought back for analysis and learning.

Support Teams need to be supported by the organization, and usually by the person to whom they report. Organizations are frequently mistrustful of teams, especially high profile teams known to be material to strategy. On the one hand teams need to be protected from this potential organizational hostility, on the other, their activities must be explained, properly presented to, and discussed with the organization at large. They must be buoyed up when they get miserable, reassured when they are in doubt, admired when they succeed, etc.

Objectives Successful teams have always translated their purpose into a series of measurable objectives. Further these objectives have been understood by each member and accepted by those responsible for the team. Measures and metrics have been set up and agreed and there is little ambiguity. True, these objectives may not emerge immediately, but once enshrined, they must direct the energy of the team.

Characteristics

Interpersonal skills Successful teams develop the ability to work together without unproductive conflict. This does not mean that they do not argue or disagree. They simply do not allow differences to disrupt the achievement of the purpose or objectives. Almost always this means that they are respectful of each other's views, open and honest in their opinions and they feel free to express differences. Nobody is made to feel small or stupid.

Partly as a consequence of good interpersonal skills, successful teams generate a high degree of participation among members. People contribute their views and experience; more importantly they contribute their time and their energy.

Participation Partly as a consequence of good interpersonal skills, successful teams generate a high degree of participation among members. People contribute their views and experience; more importantly they contribute their time and their energy. This enriches the raw material the team has to work with by providing a wider base of knowledge and active help in problem solving. Participation also implies that when team members undertake to do something, they actually do it.

Decision making Decisions are reached with a proper evaluation of the information; more, the team is good at gathering all the information. It looks at options carefully, considers consequences, is imaginative about alternatives and, at the same time, pragmatic and realistic. Members feel bound by decisions and even if they do not agree personally with them they support them in practice.

Creativity Successful teams almost always access new ideas, different ways of doing things, novel perspectives on events or circumstances. The team often develops the ability to 'jam' in the jazz sense – one idea leads to another, and another, and another . . . people build on each other's thinking and often new ground is broken.

Managing the external environment Good teams ensure that members interact with their outside world – usually the rest of the organization, so that people know what is happening in the team to the extent they need or want to. This often reduces organizational suspicion and enables a higher degree of external co-operation and fewer unwelcome surprises.

Teams and Kaizen

As with any team, nothing helps success as much as success. Being on a winning streak is probably the most cogent and effective contributor to excellent performance. To the extent that this is possible, success should be put to work to enhance the team's effectiveness.

If we compare the characteristics of effective teams above with the ten principles of *Kaizen* earlier in this chapter we see a high level of congruence. *Kaizen* illuminates a code of behaviour based on openness, surfacing problems, support and self discipline which fit closely with the observed behaviour of successful teams. Plainly this is no happy coincidence since teaming, and cross-functional teaming in particular, is the medium in which *Kaizen* is rooted. What we do have though is, from two separate sources, *Kaizen* on the one hand and considerable Western research on the other, mutually supporting analyses of effectiveness.

Having both a definition of team effectiveness and a unifying doctrine (*Kaizen*) at your disposal certainly provides the tools necessary for the manager to start the process of culture change which will facilitate the strategy. Defining the tools, however, is but a small step to the real management task of becoming expert in their application.

If the utility of these powerful tools appeals though, consider a route which starts out with a team-based development of strategy which will go some way to providing the preconditions mentioned above, notably purpose and empowerment. Facilitating the team in framing its objectives will start to help team members see that a change in behaviour is vital for the team to work effectively together. This in turn will address areas of interpersonal skills, participation and decision making.

The process of team development is not the work of a moment and later chapters in this book will tell you more about how to do it. It is as well to remember Chris Patrick's assertion in the previous chapter that it probably takes five years to introduce *Kaizen* into an organization; once there though you will have created a powerful team-based system, driven by an organizational culture capable of delivering a range of organizational strategies. This organizational model continues to be characteristic of most world-class companies.

SUMMARY

Organizational Need	Kaizen Offers
Strategic imperatives	
• Customer satisfaction	These concepts lie at the heart of Kaizen
• Continuous quality enhancement	philosophy; they are the 'cardinal
• Continuous cost reduction	virtues' – those things which Kaizen is
• Continuous employee development and learning	designed to nurture in order to produce corporate competitive advantage.
How the organization delivers the strategy	
• Productivity of synergistic teaming	Kaizen's team-based systems supported
• Cross-functional work flows	by a code of behaviour characteristic of
• Creativity in problem solving	high performing teams. Focus on the customer.
Culture which facilitates the delivery of the strategy	
• Openness and readiness to surface problems	A ready-made philosophy which has achieved wide international success and
• Focus on continuous improvement	broad application.
• Personal discipline	
• Supportive relationships	

PART TWO

Setting up and Running Kaizen Teams

CHAPTER 4

Leading the Kaizen Team: A Role Model

PATRICIA WELLINGTON

Manager, Europe Japan Centre

LEADING A KAIZEN TEAM, AND creating the environment in which it will operate and reach potential, requires multifaceted leadership skills. These skills must exist within the team and outside it. This chapter outlines the leadership competencies which need to be deployed to achieve success.

INTRODUCTION

In any study, or even any passing observation of successful *Kaizen* applications, one thing stands out clearly from the start: the leadership of each team is taken very seriously indeed.

Because it is a well documented success story for the transplantation of *Kaizen* to a Western workforce, the Toyota plant in Kentucky is alluded to more than once in this book. Team leader development practices in this highly successful plant have attracted some study and serve as an interesting example of just how seriously leadership is taken.

Most of the Kentucky workforce is composed of teams, and all performance management in the plant is handled at a team level rather than at an individual level. Teams are relatively small and there are many of them; this provides lots of opportunity for developing leadership capabilities. A team leader earns about 5 per cent more than other members; the smallness of the differential ensures that those who wish to become leaders do so overwhelmingly for reasons of personal development rather than cupidity.

Initial team leader training is a six-week programme with trainees attending daily for two-hour sessions. These sessions are run outside normal shift times and trainees attend in their own time, not the company's. Almost all team leaders will, at some time, visit Japan as well. Team meetings take place before and after each shift, the first to agree the team's objectives for the shift, the second to review how the objectives were met and what was learned.

Here, then, we have a *Kaizen* company environment in which team leader development is ongoing, highly planned and requires a major commitment from team leaders. Team operation is part of the structure, built into the operating practices, in fact inseparable from the fabric of the value chain of the company.

For many of us who are engaged in extending the use and effectiveness of teams, *Kaizen* and others, across our organizations, we do not have the luxury of Toyota's colossal experience and supportive infrastructure and so we must look to developing successful team leadership qualities. This chapter shares some advice on and experience in doing this.

THE TEAM LEADER

There are two leadership roles which are absolutely critical in successful team applications. The first, unsurprisingly, is the **internal team leader**, the person who, for want of a better word, 'chairs' the team, runs the meetings, supervises the team's processes, and who works with and in the team on a day-to-day basis.

The second is as important: it is the role of the person outside the team to whom it is usually responsible for its activities. Sometimes this person is called the **team's sponsor**. I like the American analogy; it is the person who 'rides shotgun for the team'.

In the days of the wild west, stagecoaches carried a person whose continuous responsibility it was to scan the horizon for menacing situations, hostile Indians, robbers or whatever. This person, armed of course – presumably with a shotgun – was also expected to deal with these incidents. He (while I am no expert, I assume there were few, if any, women so engaged) had no responsibility other than to assure that the stagecoach operated smoothly, did not run into trouble, was defended against attacks and so on. It has been my experience that this 'shotgun role' is crucial in setting up and operating successful teams.

Let us look at each of these leadership roles in further detail.

Tasks/responsibilities of the team leader

We need to be clear about the difference between the tasks, or responsibilities, of the leader, and the qualities or competencies he or she will have to be able to deploy in order for the team to succeed. If we look first at the tasks this might provide us with a useful generic summary.

- To assure that the team is 'on-purpose', that it is doing what it is supposed to be doing; that it is on course to achieve the reasons for its creation.
- To allocate work and resources within the team.
- To make sure that the all important team processes take place – the way members interact with each other, the way decisions are taken, the way participation is encouraged, etc.
- To ensure the flows of information into, out of, and within the team are operating well.
- To manage the time of the team effectively.

Ultimately the team leader is there to facilitate the team achieving its results or objectives.

Ultimately the team leader is there to facilitate the team achieving its results or objectives. Often the role involves framing and agreeing those objectives in the first place, as we shall see below.

Qualities and competencies

If the tasks are clear what are we able to say about the leadership competencies needed for success?

When Meredith Belbin was conducting his seminal research into teams at the Henley Management College, he framed nine roles characteristic of successful teams. He holds that if these roles are represented among team members and are being played in the team's operations the team is predisposed to success.

Belbin's nine team roles are well documented and there are psychometrics available to identify the personal characteristics of candidate team members so that, theoretically, it is possible to build a team whose members will collectively exhibit all the behaviours or roles required for success. The reality, however, is that one rarely has the luxury of being able to build a team on this basis. If you use Belbin's roles as success criteria, then you have to ensure that they are delivered by training members to incorporate them in the processes of the team's operation, rather than by relying on their inherent predisposition to the chosen behaviour.

Belbin's early work also sought to identify the qualities of a successful team leader. He sought a type, one in whom a set of specific characteristics and traits were to be found and which made that person a good leader. Starting from teams which were judged to be delivering a high level of performance, he backtracked to determine what it was the leaders were doing to facilitate the team's success. The concept of type proved elusive; he found that a wide range of behavioural patterns, competencies and strengths achieved success. He even concluded that superior intellectual ability did not necessarily make a successful leader, though if the leader could not keep up with the team, it predisposed both leader and team to failure.

More recently Belbin has provided us with a relatively simple set of guidelines for successful team leadership. While helpful, they are not, in my view, definitive. The matrix on page 62 summarizes this thinking.

You will find the matrix a useful first level guide. I say first level because in the hypercompetitive and fast changing world in which we live, the team leadership role, in common with all levels and types of organizational leadership, is changing radically. We will explore some of those changes later in this chapter.

Type of team	What the team does	Leadership capabilities needed
Operational	There primarily to improve efficiency. Such teams look to processes within their operational area to optimize them, make them more efficient, improve performance and reduce cost.	Leader needs a high degree of drive and willingness to overcome obstacles. Has to be able to convert ideas into realities and action. Needs to be able to handle the detail and tie up the loose ends.
Cross-functional	Here the team's major thrust is to work across many different functional departments within an organization to achieve improvements. Such teams might be focused on TQM for example, or on improving customer satisfaction.	Here we need a good chairperson, somebody who helps to clarify objectives and uses good decision-making techniques. Qualities of insight, diplomacy and smoothing out differences between competing functions are needed. The abilities to generate and evaluate external opportunities, and maintain a network also help.
Strategic	Here the team is focused on providing the unit or organization with long-term competitive advantage, clear differentiation in the eyes of its customers. It is dealing with future focus and a host of complex variables.	Here we need somebody with good judgement, somebody capable of navigating through complex, conflicting and inherently non-comparable data. The ability to be creative and to generate imaginative solutions helps. Personal confidence and 'groundedness' is needed.

THE SHOTGUN RIDER'S ROLE

Tasks/responsibilities

Earlier we identified the critical importance of this leadership role. If the team is to be successful the sponsor must be very successful in two major areas. The first is the preparatory work in setting up the team:

- deciding how, where and what sort of team to put in position
- recruiting/appointing the members and the team leader
- setting up the team with a clear mandate, purpose, scope and operating boundaries

- preparing, informing and reassuring the organization in which the team will operate.

Once the team is set up, the role switches to creating and managing the right environment in which the team will operate. It involves:

- procuring resources for the team
- representing the team and its interests to the rest of the organization
- guarding the team from outside attack by others in the organization
- acting as facilitator, mentor, counsellor, gopher, ambassador, adviser, feather-smoother, mediator and friend to the team.

Both Niall Foster's and Bob Hersowitz's contributions later in this book (Chapters 5 and 6 respectively) are prerequisite reading for the sponsor/shotgun rider to master. If success is to be achieved and a high performing team created, this role is absolutely crucial.

Qualities and competencies of the shotgun rider

In the early days of the team's establishment and during its formative period, the team is usually highly reliant on its sponsor and dependent upon the support, nurturing, counselling and cajoling he or she provides.

The critical need is to help the team understand its purpose in being established. This may sound naively obvious, but it has been my experience that sponsors frequently spend more time explaining WHAT is expected of the team rather than WHY it is there. The sponsor's role is to make the connection between the organization's strategic intent and the reason for the team's existence.

The sponsor's role is to make the connection between the organization's strategic intent and the reason for the team's existence.

Let us take the example above of an operational team formed to improve the processes and, say, to cut costs. This may sound like a perfectly clear mandate but it is not. It describes a set of outcomes, not a contribution to the organization's strategic intent.

Cutting costs may be a required outcome because:

- the organization is uncompetitive and will reflect the savings of cost cuts in its pricing to its customers
- the organization is not making sufficient return for its shareholders, in which case the benefit of cost savings will be reflected in dividends

- the organization needs to improve its cashflows, in which case improved margins will contribute to more positive cashflows.

The issue here is that the team's behaviour might be very different depending on what lies behind the cost cutting objective. Its order of priorities, the objectives it devises for itself, the focus of its energy will all be different depending on the strategic initiatives it is there to support.

It is the sponsor's role to make that link between team objectives and organizational strategy and to assert it continuously, unambiguously and honestly. The sponsor must be able to help the team build its vision of what successes might look and feel like quantitatively and qualitatively.

Like being a parent, the sponsor of a team which moves towards high performance must learn the skill of progressively letting go.

Evidence is that leaders who build such a vision with their teams are more effective, their teams better grounded and the results more imaginative.

Above all the sponsor must resist the idea of 'selling' the team; the skill is to facilitate the team's buying process.

A model for leadership during this forming period might look like this table.

Team's need during forming period	Supporting sponsor/shotgun-rider competence
Establishing purpose	To think, talk and present organizational strategy. Evince honesty and conviction. Debate, help unpack, tumble, clarify, explore and elucidate the team's purpose and its relationship to strategy.
Establishing a vision of success	Realize it must be the team's vision. Help facilitate the team's developing of it; 'dream' imagine, prompt, applaud, reinforce, clarify, question, help crystallize. Insert, if necessary, pragmatism and realism.
Establishing objectives	Realize they must be the team's objectives. Help them develop their objectives (these are often more demanding than any that the sponsor might lay upon them). Help them define the metrics – how will we know? Again pragmatism, realism.

Letting go

Like being a parent, the sponsor of a team which moves towards high performance must learn the skill of progressively letting go. As we have seen above the role change requires moving from involvement, active facilitation and development, to managing the environment in which the team operates.

Many leaders find that undertaking this change is surprisingly difficult and the case history is riddled with stories of how sponsors, accustomed to a high degree of executive control and decision making, feel ignored and left out when the team they have created develops the assurance to take decisions for itself. A feeling of being redundant is widely experienced. Sometimes, rather than basking in the success of the team, sponsors feel a sense of resentment at the ingratitude of the team. Here are some quotes from sponsors finding difficulty with a different role.

> *I felt that I was placed outside the perimeter fence and was peeking in to see what they were up to at any time.*

> *I'm really indignant about what they are suggesting . . . I feel they are usurping my role . . . I'm going to have to slap them back.*

> *I used to be a hunter, now I am a farmer.*

> *I feel like Dr Frankenstein – look at the monster I've created.*

Finding this new hands-off role and working to manage the environment is a precondition for the successful operation of the team though; this, together with a careful monitoring of its vital signs.

Most leaders also find (as, it must be said, do most parents) that the team sometimes hits trouble and needs intervention, redirection or therapy. In his chapter *Changing the Game – Re-directing the Kaizen Teams* (Chapter 8), John Hall outlines a technique called challenge mapping which becomes the sponsor's role when the team gets into difficulties.

THE KAIZEN PERSON

A model for leadership in the *Kaizen* context is very clearly defined by describing what has become known as the *Kaizen Person*. This person is a coach, a trainer, a motivator, a good communicator and a resource for colleagues and team members.

Kaizen, with its strong focus on process, enjoins the leader (team leader or sponsor) to focus on the processes of the team. This means that the leader manages how the team is working together. At the heart of *Kaizen* lies the conviction that if you get the process right, the results will follow close behind. If we merge the Belbin role typologies with this focus on process, we start to see two strands coming clearly together. The team processes which the leader will be managing and developing among members are generally congruent to Belbin's roles.

At the heart of the *Kaizen* leadership philosophy though lies a blend of values and behaviour which redefine the management command and control philosophies of the early management thinkers. At the risk of creating yet another list these components are:

- pride in work, in the products or services provided and in the organization that provides them
- willingness to take responsibility, to be accountable, to carry the can
- strong focus on customers and an overwhelming respect for customer preference
- close attention to detail; getting things right, believing things can always be improved upon
- a co-operative and amenable approach, able to take and offer constructive feedback and advice
- openness, honesty and integrity; the confidence and willingness to surface and confront problems
- actively supportive of colleagues, those close by and those in other parts of the organization.

There is a certain unreality in this list, a pronounced 'motherhood and apple-pie' bias which understandably attracts cynicism and dismissiveness. The argument goes that in the formal hierarchical structures of Japanese management, this kind of behaviour is sustainable; that it has become normative behaviour. To make it work in a Western management context, it is argued, people would have actually to believe in these values and that is simply incompatible with contemporary corporate realities.

The argument is not without truth, especially in the carnage of job losses, particularly white collar jobs, which has gone on across the world in the last decade and a half. Yet the evidence is that Western management is aligning itself more closely with this model. It is trying to build organizational cultures which sustain these values and demonstrate this kind of behaviour. Part of the reason for this is that organizational success is increasingly seen to reside in the ability of the employee to add value. It is possible that it is the degree to which an organization can tap into this discretionary effort of its people which most closely correlates with its success.

EMERGENT LEADERSHIP MODELS

We are witnessing, and have been for a decade, the lingering demise of a model for the management of organizations. Essentially this model arose from the brilliant strategists of the 1960s and 1970s, people like Porter, Levitt, Ohmae, etc.

The model was predicated on the premise that an organization develops a strategy to dominate given sectors of the market. This strategy gets translated into an operating plan which specifies the products and services we are going to provide, and how they are going to be differentiated from those of our competitors.

The plan is passed out to the organization to achieve. The network through which it is passed is the management structure of the organization. At a number of nodes distributed through this network, the individual managers deconstruct the plan into operating objectives which they then set about to achieve with their people. The organization monitors its compliance with the plan through the same points along the same management structure.

In this way a plan is enacted through a complex system with the managers representing the executive arm of an omniscient boardroom.

This model can no longer work because IT, globalization, and a more demanding customer have so accelerated the rate of change that the half-life of a traditional strategic plan is probably shorter than it takes for the MBAs to write it up. Michael Colenso's chapter *The Changing Strategic Environment* (Chapter 10) goes into more detail on this subject and need not be rehearsed here.

The core competence which is likely to differentiate the successful organization of the future will probably be its tactical flexibility within the context of a shared strategic direction.

What is needed now, in this rapidly changing hypercompetitive world, is a faster moving organizational system, guided and orientated by something other than the classical strategic plan, and focused more on its customers than on its compliance with the holy writ of the boardroom. The core competence which is likely to differentiate the successful organization of the future will probably be its tactical flexibility within the context of a shared strategic direction.

This has led to a new organizational model emerging. First, there are fewer management 'nodes' as organizations have become flatter. Second, a new point of reference (formerly the strategic plan) has to exist to channel the energy and activity of the organization. This point of reference is, increasingly, alignment. People in the organization plan their time, set their priorities, select their tasks on the basis of understanding the **purpose** of the organization (and their operating unit); the **vision** of the organization (and their operating unit); according to the **values** of the organization (and those of their operating unit). Further alignment is achieved by developing purpose, vision and values through participative activity. Employees don't just know about these things, they are parentally related to them.

The emerging leadership role then has moved on from coach, mentor, facilitator – all of which remain important competencies – but now the leader must be a strategist, must be able to help stimulate the creation, sharing and understanding of purpose and vision. He or she must be able to help translate this into a meaningful strategic intent, and it is this, rather than objectives, which directs and channels the discretionary effort and imagination of the people.

The 'builder binder' and fractal leadership

Roger Putt,[1] has characterized the new leader role as a 'builder binder', one who does not control the boundaries of work as managers do, but rather creates and builds alignment to the boundaries through what he calls fractal leadership. (A fractal is a geometric pattern repeated at ever smaller scales but similar nature within a system – e.g. each individual floret of a cauliflower is a replication of a total cauliflower.) To make the same point, George Ainsworth Land draws on the analogy of DNA, unique to every individual, but perfectly and completely replicated in every cell of that organism.

The essence of this thinking is that in an increasingly turbulent environment the organization will no longer have the time to plan, co-ordinate and enact a tactical response to all events. The only way it can ensure a swift but appropriate reaction is by trusting that those who deal with it are guided by a shared vision and understood strategic intent. Again the biological model is compelling; the avoidance of pain is not guided by the brain (the boardroom), but by a highly efficient subsystem, the reflex. The regeneration of damaged tissue is not directed by the brain but is handled (with total efficiency) at the cellular level.

Depowerment

Besides the concept of the builder binder and fractal leadership, Roger Putt also offers a convincing component of the new leadership model, that of depowerment. The essence of this is the transfer of power from the centre, from the leader to the coal-face where real operations are taking place. Nobody seriously questions the need to develop empowered people and teams, but this empowerment cannot take root and start to influence performance until it is supported by a matching management depowerment – see the letting go comments above.

SUMMARY

A new leadership paradigm is starting to emerge; it requires the ability to devolve control from the centre and simultaneously ensure the integrity and appropriateness of response at the periphery. The mechanisms are alignment with purpose, vision, value and strategic intent. The skills are the ability to replicate this DNA or fractal throughout the organization and to ensure the empowered response of the periphery by depowering the centre.

The structural support underpinning this new leadership model is, and will increasingly be, the team. The ability to bring the team to high performance rests on gaining alignment and on using the principles of *Kaizen* to develop the team's processes to a high degree of expertise.

The *Kaizen* person is a highly appropriate role model on which to build this new leadership role, and a *Kaizen* culture is well suited to support the behaviours which are necessary for its success.

Courageous Leadership Case Study – Unisys

The information services and technology markets were going through a bad time a few years ago – they were all trying to find new directions for the future, everyone was involved in downsizing, share prices were low, and so was staff morale.

Unisys in Europe was no exception. At times like these companies have to tighten their belts, looking for reductions in operational costs, etc. Training is usually a prime source of savings at such times.

George Cox was head of Unisys Information Services in Europe. Despite all the operational pressures – cutting costs, closing unprofitable units, refocusing and so on – George decided to invest in pulling together and strengthening the leadership skills of his senior management team, and commissioned a five-day training course for this purpose. Quite an investment of time in troubled times.

The course was so successful that it united the senior management team in a determination to drive the development of leadership skills through all levels of management in their organization. Over 300 managers attended the course during the next 12 months – and members of the top team attended the closing session of every one. During this session the attendees presented their concerns and also their suggestions for improvement – and also volunteered to pursue what they selected to be a main issue where they could make a difference – in effect, creating virtual task forces.

At a time of great pressure, when so much tough action had to be taken, George's belief in leadership skills sent a strong message throughout the organization. It demonstrated that personal development was not just a 'soft' issue, a long-term consideration to be undertaken when there was time to spare. Rather it was a vital element in tackling the immediate issues. It also showed that in turning a business around every individual has a role to play.

It worked!

Note

1. Roger Putt's work on Leadership is shortly to be generally available with the publication of *The Builder Binder* due for publication in Autumn 1999

CHAPTER 5

Setting up the Team – Preconditions for Success

Introduction

———

Essential Advice for the Team Manager

———

What do Team Members Worry About?

———

Summary

NIALL FOSTER

Associate, Europe Japan Centre

THIS CHAPTER PROVIDES A HOW-TO for setting up the team, *Kaizen* or otherwise. It gives the person responsible for setting up the team clear guidance on those things he or she will need to consider and to get right. It then focuses on the perspective of team members to help understand the dynamics of the operating team.

INTRODUCTION

H.B. Karp[1] posed the following questions to help determine whether teams and team work are appropriate.

- Do people need to work interdependently in order to meet organizational objectives, and if so, to what extent?
- Can greater employee satisfaction, higher productivity or better quality be attained through the combination of individual efforts?

If the responses to these questions are 'yes', team working can most effectively bring about the required change or improvement.

So, one-person teams don't work. A carefully co-ordinated team effort is required to achieve organizational objectives. This is a tough job. Increasing productivity and adding value/profitability to organizations which are constantly having to reinvent themselves due to the pace of change, doesn't come easy. Employees get stressed, distracted, confused. Some jockey for position, some give up. They look to *you* to 'fix things', and even those who are willing to help can't agree on *how* things should be fixed. Senior management is telling you to do more with less. 'Do it better', they say, 'it's the only way organizations survive in today's competitive marketplace'.

In this chapter we will look at a strategy that will reduce risks, protect productivity and retain the team spirit necessary to achieve high performance and realize the team's objectives quickly and decisively. What follows is a practical guide and a review of the advice necessary for the *Kaizen* manager about how to co-ordinate team effort, set direction, targets, goals and purpose for the team. Understanding these things will help you monitor your own performance and that of your team.

ESSENTIAL ADVICE FOR
THE TEAM MANAGER

1. Confront reality

Your first priority is creating the team, a team that can work through the changes required. Your job is to orchestrate a carefully co-ordinated group effort and mobilize people against the threats to high performance. You must concentrate on engineering the individual efforts of the team into a unified, coherent, collective effort. You will have to create a team culture and team language relevant to the job in hand. The reality is that your reputation is at stake. The best way to protect that reputation is to get results.

2. Empower yourself

To get results you must move with authority, make decisions, act. You must consciously influence and use your power. You can't mobilize others if you're immobilized yourself. You won't achieve anything without 'power' and if you can't do anything, why are you in charge? People will not follow someone they don't believe in and they won't believe in you unless you believe in yourself.

3. Take charge

Don't act tentatively in the early stages of constructing your team. Take charge and make things happen. Your effectiveness depends heavily on your credibility with your team members and you undermine that credibility when you wallow or waffle. People will not rally behind a manager they can't respect. Don't confuse respect with popularity. Focus on getting results. Do what needs to be done. Ensure that you solicit other people's opinions because that puts you in a position to wield authority in an informed manner. Everyone has a voice, but you call the shots. Consensus management is great if you have time, but today it is often too slow a process. Take charge without being a bully. *Sell* benefits persuasively rather than only tell, admit mistakes when you make them, and press on. Make sure your team believes in you.

4. Set a clear agenda

Team members need a clear sense of direction *quickly*. How else can they be effective as a team? Clear priorities help team members to figure out how to spend their time. The action plan sets out the agenda with crystal-clear tactical objectives giving the team laser-like focus. Alignment of effort depends on your ability to orientate the team and orchestrate a co-ordinated effort. Map out new priorities. Keep them simple and tie them to a specific timetable. Set short-term goals that the team can achieve quickly. Potential resistance can be defused when your instructions are unequivocal and easily understood. Make known your commitment to them and their commitment to achieving the goals. Tell them at the outset that they can expect some mid-course corrections. The agenda will have to be adapted as the situation demands it. But, *always* keep it clear and communicate it constantly.

Of course, key team members can contribute to designing the team's priorities and objectives. You must consider their input. The more they can shape the agenda, the more buy-in and commitment they'll show. Plus, their ideas might dramatically improve your sense of priorities. In the final analysis, though, *you* remain accountable.

5. Focus on concrete results

With the pace of change accelerating, many employees change their attitude towards their organization. During times of change, which may be seen as upheaval by some, trust levels often drop. Morale slips. Loyalty withers. Job stress rises. As the person in charge, you had better take these emotional matters seriously. Strong feelings influence the way people behave. What all this means is that your job gets harder. These emotional intangibles must not become your top priority, however. Instead, focus on problems, not symptoms. How can you build trust? Simply be trustworthy in the way that you and your team pursue your goals. Focus on tangible results. Go for those operational improvements that are most urgently needed. Focus on those things that go straight to the bottom line or that contribute directly to competitive position. Stake out specific targets. Aim for a few – but ambitious – goals. Go for measurable gains. *Kaizen* is a results-oriented strategy and indirectly it does the most to improve employee attitudes. If you focus on fighting the causes of your team's aches and pains and get rid of root problems, watch the 'emotional' symptoms disappear.

6. Know your team

The casting of people – determining who goes, who stays and who goes where – carries a lot of weight. Put people in the right place to begin with, and you won't be forced to make shifts later on. New challenges rewrite job descriptions. So start from scratch in analyzing your available people assets. Approach the exercise as if all team members were 'new hires'. Check for people's adaptability. Ask yourself who is best suited for which role. If there are weak players whom you must use, position them where they'll hurt the team least. Size up your team with a dispassionate, discerning eye. You need good data, and you need it in a hurry. You can't afford to sit back and figure out your team members as the months go by. You need to make informed judgements *now*. If you don't trust your skills at this, or if you feel that you just can't make the time, get help.

Put people in the right place to begin with, and you won't be forced to make shifts later on.

Look for strengths, weaker points, aspirations and work preferences. Look for experience and areas of expertise. Look for concerns and points of resistance. The sharper your insights into each individual, the better the odds that you'll manage him or her effectively.

7. Keep your best people

Your key people can be the cornerstones of your team effort, so don't take these people for granted. *Re-recruit* them. Make *everyone* feel important. Invest the same time and effort in creating the team that you would in recruiting a new employee. Try to capture people's spirit. Put some fire into their feeling about the work in hand. Ensure they're on board *emotionally*. Successful team work depends heavily on your ability to stabilize the group. Try to keep it intact throughout the project.

Invest the same time and effort in creating the team that you would in recruiting a new employee.

8. Ensure roles and responsibilities are understood

Ensure everyone knows what is expected of them. Don't leave people to work things out on their own. Get rid of rule ambiguity. Nail down each team member's responsibilities with clarity, precision and attention to detail.

There must be no question of where one job stops and the next one starts. Leave no blur regarding the responsibilities each team member is supposed to shoulder. Work out precisely what needs to be done, who's going to do which part of it, and communicate your plan. Give every team member a brief job description. State your expectations regarding standards of performance. Describe the chain of command in the team. Outline each person's spending limits, decision-making authority, and reporting requirements. Everyone will be best served if you put this information down in writing.

Check to make sure that each team member understands the team's (whole) set-up and how it fits together. Be careful to avoid job overlap, since that feeds power struggles, wastes resources and frustrates everyone involved. When explaining to people what to do, also specify what they should *not* do. Differentiate between crucial tasks and peripheral, low priority activities. Spell out what needs to be accomplished in each position and for what the person will be held most accountable. Once you have done this, pay attention to what team members are doing. Keep everyone on track. If you see something going wrong, fix it immediately.

9. Be urgent

The team manager's role is to energize the team, mobilize it and to keep additional change from choking off its energy. You need to show a strong sense of urgency. Seriously consider what your work habits are conveying to the team. Are you putting in extra hours? What about your personal productivity? Does your behaviour show a burning job commitment? Without a sense of urgency, you can't function as the pivotal influence around which the members coalesce into a team. Like it or not, you are the role model and team members take their cue from you.

Keep the pressure on for productivity. Set tight deadlines. Push for quicker decisions. Expedite. Operate with a bias for action. Let everybody know that you will be tolerant of honest mistakes, but intolerant of inaction and inertia. Praise those who are energetic. Nip at the heels of those who drag their feet.

Instead of patiently planning and preparing, just get going. Move immediately to make measurable results as soon as possible. Start with the resources you've got. Start with an attacking strategy, score quickly and start building momentum. Inertia is your big enemy right now.

10. Tighten discipline

High performance teams are disciplined. The team members are strict with themselves and they execute with precision. People play for the team – not just for themselves – and are intolerant of half-hearted effort. These teams are self-policing. They deal swiftly with members who disregard the team's rule system, whether those rules are written down or just implicitly agreed by all.

The team leader must function as the main disciplinary agent for the team. Start by setting high standards. Then defend them. Aim for excellence to build pride, *esprit de corps* and cohesiveness. Keep things tightly organized. Don't allow people to drift back into old routines or habits. Hold team members accountable for all their assigned tasks. Keep them to their agreed timetables and deadlines. Don't be vague or fuzzy in laying down the rules, or in explaining what you want, or inconsistent in enforcing objectives. If you make as many exceptions as you do rules, you have no rules. Always be prepared to back up your words with action. Team members will listen to what you have to say, but their behaviour will be shaped by what you *do*. Keep a high profile. Remember that you have no more powerful way to communicate than by example. You can't lead by example if the team can't see you. This way team members will have confidence in you.

Team members will listen to what you have to say, but their behaviour will be shaped by what you do.

11. Compliment and praise

Reward, reward and reward good performance. The intangible rewards you have to offer are limitless. Words of encouragement, compliments, empathy and understanding, a note of appreciation. Stopping to share a cup of coffee, or taking a team member to lunch. Giving team members special assignments or more decision-making authority. Saying a sincere thank you, asking about the family, celebrating small victories, soliciting opinions and suggestions – the whole gamut of interpersonal skills will help. Try listening, really listening, a smile, a warm handshake or pat on the back. Try taking others into your confidence; asking team members for help is gratifying because it validates one's worth.

Caring takes time. It requires that you pay attention to what's happening. Create a supportive team environment – nurture – and watch it bring out the best in people. Show approval and see how it arms the

If you make every member of the team feel special, you'll end up with a very special team.

team. When you affirm, you empower. People feel safer, valued and more optimistic. Trust levels increase. Team members are more creative and engage their talents more fully. If you make every member of the team feel special, you'll end up with a very special team.

12. Ensure communication flows

Give the team constant updates. Even no news is news. If you don't regularly update the team, they'll fill in the blanks themselves and you feed the rumour mill by default. Unless you speak for yourself, somebody will speak for you. If you want certain information to stick, keep saying it. If you have to deliver a complex or difficult message, put it in writing.

Since communication travels four times as fast from the top down as from the bottom up, you should put new 'pipelines' in place to carry information to you. If you know what the problems are and hear about them early enough, you can usually fix them. So deputize every team member. Ask them to go looking for problems. Instead of looking for proof that changes are happening or working, search for evidence that they are not.

Bring your team together often. Talk. Air issues and discuss. Pool everyone's thoughts on how to resolve problems so as to keep everyone 'in the loop'. Invite argument and allow conflict. You'll end up with better solutions. Don't allow differences to be swept under the carpet as this will haunt the team later. You won't have a high performance team unless you meet the tough issues head-on.

13. Point your team in one direction

Teams need to know where they're going. Team members perform best when they unite with a keen sense of mission, knowing they're heading somewhere special. If the aiming point is clear and the vision is compelling, it draws the team together and pulls them forward. Concentrate on making the vision a *cause*.

Teams get fired up about crusades and not about 'strategic plans'. Give the team a sense of purpose that captures their imagination and encourages them to close ranks.

Co-ordinate team effort by explaining explicitly the specific results the team is expected to achieve. You must believe in what the team is doing. If not, how can you defend it, sell it and turn the vision into reality? True leaders, true visionaries, do everything to control events. Team managers must become true leaders. True leaders are driven by a vision, every team member must be part of that vision, and that vision must encompass the individual visions of every team member. Nothing leads to disillusionment more quickly than when a team feels that it cannot change or implement what it is supposed to change.

'I have a dream!' was Martin Luther King's sales message. He certainly had a dream and by pulling out the essence and distilling it into a few clear, crisp paragraphs, he told everyone prepared to listen. This dream was underpinned by a great, overarching, simplicity: 'make Americans equal'. Like most of the best visions his was simple.

Simplicity has the benefit of being easily communicated and remembered. Team visions, too, must be simple and describe what the team is supposed to achieve in the given time span. To do this they must satisfy 'the three Rs'; they must be:

- **relevant** to the organization and its present situation
- **realistic** and achievable
- **robust** and not collapse in the face of setbacks.

14. Pay attention to process

High performance teams always pay attention to process. Think of this as your team's gearbox, the internal machinery of how it goes about its business. Destabilized teams need to be self-monitoring, or self-correcting. But during times of change or transition, team members are notorious for side-stepping or overlooking the problems of group process. Most team members look out for themselves rather than for the team. Team members are so busy 'doing' that they don't take time to evaluate *how* they're doing it. Sometimes they lack confidence in the team's ability to handle the stress of self-analysis, so they don't force the issue. The result? Nobody calls attention to dysfunctional process.

As the person in charge, the team manager should focus attention on process. What's going on inside the team? Analyze its effectiveness. Determine what's missing, what's getting in the way, what needs to happen. You need a sharp eye plus the nerve to make the team deal with process problems. Regularly stop the team in its tracks. Call a halt long enough to let the team hold a mirror up to itself.

Process analysis is as simple as saying: 'Let's look at what's going on now. How do you feel about that? Let's analyze how we're working together as a team.' Make everybody take a hard look at what's happening. Don't let people dodge issues, gloss over sensitive points, or turn the conversation toward mere chit-chat. Make the team face the facts and come up with constructive ideas on how to handle the process problems. Finally, make it clear that each team member is in charge of protecting team process. Tell everyone to throw the spotlight of attention on behaviour that gets in the way.

15. Make the team holographic

Your role is to make the team *synchronous*. This means that everybody understands that change is accepted for all the other team members as well as for oneself. Essentially, teams work very well when individuals don't worry about their personal gain. The first condition for good teamwork is that each member of the team is aware that he or she **alone** is responsible for the whole. It is not shared responsibility, it is the responsibility for everything on the shoulders of each one. The team manager's goal is to realize a *holographic* team. If you take a holographic image of a house and cut this image into pieces, you find the image of the house on each piece. The state of mind of each team member reflects the state of mind of the whole team. This is the definition of your team's spirit.

WHAT DO TEAM MEMBERS WORRY ABOUT?

From the team members' perspective, what are the priorities? Do they feel that there is a purpose to this? Does each individual have a clear sense of direction that is tied to a specific timetable? Assuming a positive or negative answer, how can team members then monitor and adjust their own performance to ensure they stay on track?

Jack R. Gibb's research on group behaviour[2] together with Arthur Young's process theories[3] contributed the view that people bring the following four basic concerns to all social interactions that can be adapted to team performance.

1. **Acceptance concerns** about the formation of trust, acceptance of oneself and others, anxiety and how to decrease it and confidence and how to increase it. Acceptance concerns primarily relate to issues of membership.

2. **Data concerns** about the communication of perceptions, feelings and ideas to team members and about the social norms of how they should be expressed.

3. **Goal formation concerns** about goal setting, problem solving and decision making and about resolving different motivations. Productivity, fun, creativity learning and growing are considered part of goal setting.

4. **Control concerns** about the regulation, co-ordination and sequencing of activities.

Young's conclusions indicated that team unity is found by appreciating the nature of processes and, together with Gibb's findings, the team-performance model was created. This found that as a newly formed team defines its work and makes choices, boundaries and restrictions are created. Teams that are successful in resolving their basic concerns appear to achieve the most freedom. High performance is associated with breaking the boundaries of individual capacity.

What follows is a study of how teams can explore their limits and monitor what they must do to stay on track and break the boundaries of individual capacity. We address eight primary elements, each representing a set of concerns that team members face when they work together. If team members can answer the questions contained in each element, questions which we regard as self-monitoring, the team has a greater chance of being successful.

1. Orientation into the team

The issues here are membership and acceptance. The core question is '*Why am I here?*' Each person who joins the team must answer this question in order to begin the process of finding his or her niche. Later, the core question becomes, 'Do I belong here?'

Team members then normally ask themselves, '*Do I want to be here?*' They must believe that the team's objectives are valuable in order that they buy fully into the team's mission. They must also believe that the team can do its work or tasks well. Finally, they must believe that their skills will be used, that they will be heard, that their being there matters and that they have some power to influence the team's direction and results.

2. The quest for meaning

Meaning refers to a value, having a sense of value, worth, fulfilment, satisfaction, respect or success. Value comes from an understanding of an activity and the achievement that comes from it. Meaning answers the question: what is something good for? All team members want to understand: '*Why this effort? Why this work, action or activity? What do I get out of it? What value do I derive from doing it? What value do others derive from this work, action or activity?*' If we were to ask team members to write down their rate of interest in their participation in their team what would many write? The objective should be 'this interests and excites me'.

3. Building trust

The main question here is '*Who are you?*', the hidden concern here is '*What will you expect of me?*' Many questions, too, need to be answered about team members. '*Are they reliable? Are they good at what they do? Are they dedicated to their work? Do they have hidden agendas?*' Being able to answer these questions affirmatively builds team trust.

4. Objectives and role clarification

During this stage, team members are primarily concerned with issues such as identifying options and managing the accompanying decisions. The purpose of creating the team in the first place is that it gets somewhere. Individual team members will be asking themselves '*What must I do, how and by when?*' and considering the 'contract' with the team manager will want to know '*How should I behave in the team and with the team manager?*'

5. Commitment

The team is now ready to take action. The core questions are '*How?*' and '*Which way?*' During this phase the team chooses the directions and divides responsibilities.

6. Implementation

The key questions are '*How should things be done? Who is doing what, when and where?*' The sequencing and scheduling of work is a major concern here.

7. High performance

'*How can we create harmony and excitement in the team? Which aspects of my work require the highest levels of performance?*' Ideally, each team member believes that he or she is essential to the work effort and feels responsible for his or her contributions.

8. Renewal

At the renewal stage the key question is '*Why continue?*' This allows team members to examine their jobs and to ask themselves whether the task in hand suits their lifestyles and their career plans. To a certain extent this stage is similar to the orientation stage. Team members are trying to assess where they are, why they are there and what now needs to be done. Positive responses to these questions usually energize the questioners and renew their sense of commitment. Negative answers, on the other hand, indicate an unwillingness to continue.

SUMMARY

Managing the formation and development of the team requires energy, consistency of behaviour and a solid appreciation of team dynamics. When the result is high performance, the reward for manager and team alike is a level of fulfilment and satisfaction which usually far exceeds mere personal satisfaction.

Notes

1.   Karp, H.B. (1976) *A Gestalt approach to collaboration in organizations*

2.   Bradford, Gibb and Benne (1964) *T-group theory and laboratory method*

3.   Young, A. (1976) *The geometry of meaning and the reflexive universe*

CHAPTER 6

Self Management and the Kaizen Team – Empowerment versus Tasking

ROBERT HERSOWITZ

Associate, Europe Japan Centre

After defining a self-managing team, the author goes on to outline the requirements for their success. Taking a practical how-to-get-going approach the author outlines the stages in setting them up and then helps the reader understand their function by dealing with each of the phases of their development.

INTRODUCTION

The concept of self-managing teams grew out of the Deming-inspired Japanese school of management in the 1970s. It followed on from an emphasis on quality circles. The main difference between quality circles and self-managing teams is the fact that quality circles were designed for temporary cross-functional activity whilst self-managing teams are more permanent and have a longer life span. They are more closely associated with *Kaizen* because they seek to perpetuate continuous improvement for the team. So what is a self-managed team? It is important to understand what is meant by the term. The established consensus view is that a self-managed team is:

a highly trained group of between 6 to 18 people on average, fully responsible for turning out a well-defined segment of finished work.

The 'well-defined work' element is important. It can be a series of definable processes, e.g. building an entire motor car (Rover) or it can be something less complex, e.g. the processes involved in building a component for a motor car (Perkins Engines). Self-managing teams (SMTs) can also be made to work in service or administration environments – e.g. processing insurance claims (AXA Sunlife).

The main ethos of SMTs is the empowerment factor – where the team learns through a series of key stages, to manage itself. Organizations which are contemplating the road to self management need to understand that there are some important culture change issues that need to be considered. Many organizations have abandoned the effort of introducing SMTs because they have failed to measure themselves against a checklist of requirements before starting out. The following are the requirements needed for success.

REQUIREMENTS FOR THE INTRODUCTION OF SELF-MANAGING TEAMS

1. Full backing from the top

This is crucial. Wherever SMTs have been successful there has always been evidence of full senior management support and no lip service. Many companies would like to claim that they have introduced SMTs, but few manage to support the culture change by genuinely 'walking the talk' from the very top downwards.

2. A climate of experimentation and innovation

SMTs flourish where there is the spirit of adventure. This is not simply to do with introducing them for the sake of being different. They should be introduced with sound logical motives of improvement and gain.

3. Management–employee openness

Another crucial factor is a climate of trust between employers and staff at subordinate levels. This promotes maximum credibility for the SMTs' programme and ensures that everyone will be committed.

4. Free access to and sharing of information

This is one of the key principles of *Kaizen*. Establishing trust and openness in an organization also brings with it a willingness to share information with everyone. This fosters empowerment especially where the information can lead to people using the information to add value and become creative.

5. Union inclusion

Where an organization is unionized, then the unions need to be brought on board. This is part of establishing a climate of trust and openness. Without union support in a unionized environment, SMTs are usually doomed to fail.

6. Sufficient resources – funding, time and technology

This is one of the great challenges of the present age. Both time and resources are scarce commodities for most organizations these days. A tightly run ship, however, can improve productivity and profitability with the help of SMTs.

7. Support for training

This is linked to the previous issue of resources. SMTs do not evolve on their own. They have to be nurtured and groomed. Part of this process involves extensive training that also has to be paid for.

8. Work processes that are conducive to team working

Kaizen emphasizes the importance of process improvement through teamwork. Not every type of operation is conducive to SMTs or teamwork. The main criteria for assessing feasibility for introducing SMTs centre around the definition we've already considered, i.e.

> *a highly trained group of between 6 to 18 people on average, fully responsible for turning out a well-defined segment of finished work.*

If there are no clearly defined work segments, or if the organization is too diffuse and individuals work remotely, SMTs may not be the appropriate productivity vehicle.

9. The availability of support and assistance

Like any new change management project, the establishment of SMTs requires support. Sometimes this support may come from within, from those who have studied and helped to set up the programme. In many other instances, outside help is sought from suitable experts with good track records in introducing SMTs.

OTHER CONSIDERATIONS BEFORE INTRODUCING SELF-MANAGING TEAMS

In addition to the nine-point checklist above, there are also a number of further criteria that must be examined when considering the move towards SMTs.

Current economic climate

A number of organizations have resorted to SMTs as a way of coping with the effects of change such as mergers, downsizing or recession. In most cases these have failed. In order to make SMTs work, the organization needs to be in a fit economic state.

Can managers transform their style from 'hands on' to 'hands off'?

Apart from staff being ready and able to accept the challenges of self management, there must also be a willingness and flexibility within the managerial hierarchy to embrace and adopt an empowering way of managing. Managers have to become catalysts and change agents rather than change drivers.

Apart from staff being ready and able to accept the challenges of self management, there must also be a willingness and flexibility within the managerial hierarchy to embrace and adopt an empowering way of managing.

Employee readiness and capability

The implementation of SMTs carries with it a new and often better way of working. Most employees are not well informed about the 'why, what and how' of the self-managing system. They need to be informed and encouraged. There are instances where staff are not capable of making the adjustment.

Are work processes compatible with SMTs?

Another consideration is whether the actual work of the group or team lends itself to the self-managing concept. Conceptual work or work involving a high degree of reactive flexibility may not suit the SMT culture.

Sustaining the SMT culture throughout the organization

Some companies have successfully introduced SMTs in a 'green field' site as part of an experiment, which inevitably proves successful. Once the success has been celebrated, the next stage usually involves introducing SMTs to other locations at 'brown field' sites. In a number of cases, the success of the green field site proves threatening, resulting in the dismantling of the newly-built SMT!

The impact of self management on home and family

No culture change can be effected in isolation. Work changes affect individuals and create a whole new lifestyle. During the earliest stages of implementation there may be increased stress levels. In many cases, the introduction of SMTs may lead to extra hours or overtime. In some cases, the changes may produce more leisure time to be spent at home. Staff need the support of their families and indeed the entire community, especially where self management is being introduced in a local enterprise or factory where many town residents are employed.

INTRODUCING SELF-MANAGING TEAMS: A FIVE-STAGE PROCESS

Stage one – nominating an executive steering committee

The route to self management is a key cultural change issue and as such, needs the support and backing of top management.

The route to self management is a key cultural change issue and, as such, needs the support and backing of top management. One way of involving top management from the outset is to nominate an Executive Steering Committee. This group of people may include the Chief Executive, his or her directors and anyone else whose contribution can add value, e.g. a quality assurance executive or an executive from HR.

The purpose of the executive steering committee is to:

- become familiar with the concept of SMTs
- acquire knowledge and information about SMTs
- establish credibility for the SMT programme.

Those taking part need to educate themselves by networking, reading, attending conferences or training sessions on the subject of SMTs and/or empowerment. They need to understand the language of SMTs so that they can communicate the relevant details and influence co-workers, staff, customers and even suppliers.

Stage two – appointment and selection of a design committee

Once the steering committee has completed its initial investigation into SMTs, there is a need to appoint a design committee. Those who serve on the committee must become the drivers or project managers of the SMT programme. They must be well versed in the strategy and *phases of development* (see later, page 99) of SMTs. The design committee can be made up of two or more people. In some organizations, this may be the managing director, human resources director and the production director. In other organizations, the constituents of the design committee could be made up of a wider group of people including some line managers.

The job of the design committee is to tailor the SMT programme to suit the organization and its culture. They design the initial cultural change blueprint. They may also take part in identifying suitable groups of people and nominating the key players.

Stage three – selection of a green field site

One of the functions of the design committee is to determine the most appropriate way of introducing SMTs. This also includes the identification of a green field site. The green field site option is a good way to kick off SMTs. When the Japanese export their management culture, they believe in the concept of always starting a new idea in an unspoilt environment with people who have not been tainted by traditionalist 'Western' hierarchical work practices. By choosing a new group of people in a highly suitable part of the company, the chances of success and a quick win will increase. The design committee has to decide on some of the details. They might ask themselves the following questions as part of their feasibility study.

- Why do we want to start a self-managing team in this part of the organization?
- What are we expecting to be the result at the end? (Quantify where possible.)
- Have we assessed the actual tasks and skills in terms of the suitability for turning this group into a self-managing team?
- Who should we choose to facilitate team sessions?
- Who should be the co-ordinator?
- Does the co-ordinator have the appropriate skills?
- Are we familiar with current performance data?

Stage four – launching an induction and familiarization campaign

Once the idea of moving into SMTs has been decided, it is important for the corporate communication wheels to begin turning. Everyone needs to be informed and persuaded. This avoids rumour-mongering and paranoia. The campaign should attempt to inform and educate staff, customers, suppliers, contractors and anyone who will be affected by the introduction of SMTs. The campaign may address the following questions.

- Why are we doing this?
- What does it involve?
- What is the background and track record of SMTs in other similar organizations?
- What are the benefits and paybacks?
- How long will it take?
- What are the pitfalls?
- What are some of the people issues?
- How will this affect people's jobs?
- Who will be involved and in what way?
- What potential is there for the organization to improve, grow and strengthen itself?
- How is this all going to happen?

The design committee should have thought about all these questions. The answers should be turned into a succinct presentation that is clear and comprehensible. Written material that is brief, well pitched and graphically appealing should be printed and distributed in conjunction with effective presentations and question and answer sessions. In some successful campaigns, a 'self-managing team house style package' was developed complete with posters, videos, a logo and memorable graphics. The design committee may co-opt suitably qualified and talented people to help them in this quest.

Stage five – identification of key players

There are normally five constituent 'people' elements when launching into SMTs.

Managers These are individuals who hold conventional managerial responsibility and are drawn from the hierarchical culture of the organization. Their role is to become transformed from traditional vertical managers to enablers, leaders, coaches and sponsors of the SMT programme.

Facilitators These are neutral, objective individuals who are chosen for their process consulting skills. They know how to conduct brainstorms, to lead workshops, to act as filters and balancers of information during group discussions. They may have had previous experience in introducing *Kaizen* or quality initiatives. They may also have to act as arbitrators in times of conflict between managers and team players. They should be unbiased in their views and opinions, seeking only to clarify and monitor the communication processes. They must exhibit good leadership ability by being good listeners, good interpreters, scribes and assertive communicators. Where possible, managers should not be made facilitators of their immediate subordinate teams. Managers may act as facilitators of other teams who are not under their charge.

Team leaders These are very often the department supervisors who play the traditional line supervisor role. Team leaders are also drawn from the ranks of subordinates. Sometimes the supervisors are too addicted to old-style leadership practices and new blood must be found from amongst the ranks of subordinates. The team leaders must work with managers and facilitators and help them to shape the team. They must be supporters of the SMT concept and be prepared to act as champions and sponsors. They must also be prepared to relinquish power as self management and leadership rotation spontaneously begins to emerge.

Team players These are the members of the team who share a common goal or purpose. They create the fabric of SMTs because they **are** the team. They must be trained and developed to assume the special skills and responsibilities of self management.

Support groups These are clusters of individuals who work with the SMT. They may provide the SMT with a service – e.g. the HR department. Often they are made up of people who work in the finance and administration sector of the company. Support groups may themselves be formed into SMTs but this is not necessarily always the case. They must learn about self management in order to understand and anticipate the needs of their internal customers who are the SMTs.

ENABLING EMPLOYEES
TO BECOME SELF MANAGED

Most organizations are not ready to move into a self-managed culture. There is a need to provide training and with the training, different 'skill sets'. These include:

- technical skills
- administrative skills
- interpersonal skills.

Technical skills

This is a fundamental part of laying the foundations for self management. It begins after a thorough skills analysis where jobs are process mapped and accurately analyzed. The end result of this exercise will allow all technical and specialist skills to be identified and logged. These need to be documented and translated into performance management terminology. This can later be used for individual and team performance evaluation. It will also contribute to cross-training (multi-skilling) where team members are taught to do each other's jobs and more. This creates the fabric for a fluid matrix, 'spaghetti' or 'fishnet' organization structure. These new structures will enhance the organization's potential for maximum flexibility.

Administrative skills

These skills are crucial for the smooth running of all work/team units. Traditionally, administrative skills were part of a blue collar/white collar split. Traditional companies encouraged a kind of skilling apartheid where manual workers and technical jobholders were encouraged to leave the administrative work to the headworkers. All this is counterproductive to self-managed working. Everyone should be taught how to use computers, to record and access information. A key skill element is the ability to report procedures (writing) which is crucial for interfacing with the larger organization as well as with customers and suppliers. In addition, team players should be taught basic financial awareness and skills, which include procedures for budgeting. In many organizations there is also a need for staff to acquire simple project management skills for scheduling work and processes. This is very much a part of *Kaizen* where team players are taught how to use tools such as *Ishikawa*, to analyze, measure or plan for process improvements. In some organizations, team players are even encouraged to learn about how to hire and evaluate new team members.

Interpersonal skills

In some ways, this is probably the most important area of skill development. Most of us absorb and assimilate these skills informally. We learn from our role models (parents, teachers and bosses); we certainly are not taught appropriate skills for communicating in a self-managed culture. The key interpersonal skills required for SMTs are:

- the ability to listen and provide feedback (facilitation skills)
- group problem solving and brainstorming
- skills involving conflict management and resolution
- the ability to persuade and influence others assertively
- the ability to present ideas, information and solutions clearly and articulately
- collaborative decision making within and amongst teams
- collaboration skills – getting, sending and using information.

THE PHASES OF DEVELOPMENT OF SELF-MANAGED TEAMS

A team can be compared to any living organism. Like most organisms, teams pass through a series of development phases. Where SMTs have been developed and built, there are some clear characteristics that distinguish each phase of growth towards maturity. The phases of development for SMTs can be summarized as follows:

Phase 1: Forming

Phase 2: Chaos or storming

Phase 3: Leader-dependent

Phase 4: Closed ranks

Phase 5: Self-managed or totally empowered start-up

Phase one: forming

This phase includes all the pre-work by the executive steering committee. The groundwork also means establishing the ethos for the move towards SMTs and, as such, a mission statement and plan (outcomes) must be drafted. The forming phase also requires the selection of initial work team sites as well as support lobbying of senior and middle managers and interface contacts. All of this is accompanied by a vague allocation of roles within the initial team or teams.

During the forming phase team members:

- learn the basics of communication and interpersonal skills
- begin using administration skills (with coaching)
- learn to expand their repertoire of technical skills

and supervisors learn how to change their behaviour and become 'facilitators'.

Phase two: chaos or storming

Like most groups of people who are exposed to change, there is a degree of predictable chaos involved. This is normal and almost a necessary part of the evolution of the SMT.

Because of the predictability of this phase, it is important to inform people of what to expect. This can be achieved through informal coaching and counselling. The raising of awareness about the chaos phase can also be introduced during the forming phase. The chaos phase introduces a new group dynamic to the team. The team leader's authority fades and this forces collaborative decision making to take place. Different cultures adapt differently to this phase. In Japan and Scandinavia, groups respond well to this transition because they are surrounded by a work ethic that identifies strongly with participation and interdependence. In Britain, the transition is more difficult, mainly because of the inherent dependency on a boss culture (them and us) which has been perpetuated by the class system for so many years.

The chaos phase may also raise anxiety about job security with some of the managers. They become unwilling observers to the change in the balance of power. At this stage no one can see the benefits and positive aspects of self management and everything seems threatening. Those individuals who are not part of a team or are not candidates for the self managing culture express their opposition. Sometimes in unionized organizations, there is overt and covert resistance towards self management. Many secretly hope that the transition to SMTs will fail and that the idea will be abandoned.

Phase three: leader-dependent

By this phase, confidence grows within the team, as individuals identify with the common goals. There is a great sense of satisfaction as everyone masters new skills. People are less conscious of the differences that separate them. They become more united and motivated. They look to an internal 'natural' leader who usually emerges. The team informally nominates this person to represent them and interface with the organization. This usually means that one team member steps forward as the primary source of direction, liaison and information gatherer for the team. He or she becomes a temporary team leader who clarifies work assignments and acts as internal referee.

A fatal combination is a team of weaker individuals and one strong over-assertive personality who creates learned helplessness within the team.

The temporary leader also becomes a coach. He or she may provide counselling or informal training wherever it is needed within the group. The emergence of a temporary team leader is a natural part of any team's development. This is part of a healthy transition for the team provided that the temporary leader does not get addicted to his or her role. A newly developing SMT can also become too reliant on the temporary leader's leadership. A fatal combination is a team of weaker individuals and one strong over-assertive personality who creates learned helplessness within the team. One way of preventing this is to force the team to begin rotating the leadership role at specific intervals.

During this phase, more trust develops between the team and its manager. This is because the manager begins to see the progress which the team is making. The team begins to establish its own patterns and norms for meetings and communication with internal clients, managers and team support staff. Efficiency and productivity expand remarkably, allowing managers to remove themselves from their past 'hands on' role.

Phase four: closed ranks

By now the new culture of the SMT has taken root. In many cases, the team experiences a sense of euphoria about their ability to achieve. This is because they have learnt to identify, manage and improve their work processes whilst also meeting challenging targets. The team may easily develop an unrealistic sense of what it can achieve. The term failure becomes an anathema. Intense team spirit can lead to cover-ups of poor performance by team members. Any conflict within the team can be concealed by conscious or unconscious denial behaviour.

One of the most challenging aspects of developing SMTs is the impact of change in the organization. Change brought about through mergers, acquisitions or downsizing, leads to team tampering by management. This has a very detrimental effect on the newly emerging SMT. The team cannot come to terms with members leaving or being replaced or added. This is one reason why isolated attempts at developing SMTs proves less successful in the short term. The more widespread the inception of SMTs, the more flexibility there will be within the organization.

Pitfalls of the closed ranks phase

- At this stage, SMTs can easily develop a sense of superiority. Often this is justified because of their success and achievements.

- SMTs can become critical and resentful when the rest of the organization fails to meet their needs.

- When more than two or three SMTs are launched in one organization, fierce competition between teams can develop. If the culture change is *not* pre-empted and dealt with by management, this may lead to unhealthy 'intra-team' behaviour such as withholding information or even attempts to sabotage another team's progress.

The culture change process which surrounds the development of SMTs must include an initiative by management to create mechanisms through which all teams are constantly reminded of the organization's interdependence and collaborative working practices. A practical example of this would be the establishment of councils of elected intra-team members who monitor and evaluate how the teams are working and collaborating. The Banking Team at Sunlife developed this approach in its attempt to maintain credibility for its work within the greater, more conservative, organization.

The culture change process which surrounds the development of SMTs must include an initiative by management to create mechanisms through which all teams are constantly reminded of the organization's interdependence and collaborative working practices.

Phase five: self-managed teams

This phase is reached when the team comes of age and develops into a powerful committed body of individuals who share a common goal, understand each other's styles and work processes and are unconsciously competent in all that they do. Leadership comes from within the centre of the team. Everyone assumes ownership of team and organization goals. The real thrill of the SMT is when individuals begin to act like company owners. Each team member feels a passionate need to succeed. The culture of *Kaizen* permeates every activity as improvements are introduced, enhanced and perfected.

The focus becomes the customer. People talk about how to establish new markets or how to beat the competition. Issues that would never have been the concern of staff members in the previous hierarchical culture now become discussed as part of everyday communication. A BBC documentary about empowerment cited examples of Land Rover in the UK Midlands, where a member of an SMT would voluntarily begin work at 5.00 a.m. in order to devise, design and complete a new work process which would save the organization £30,000 in one year.

SMTs create a vital loop of information and feedback. All team members are constantly learning and acquiring new skills and competencies. They voluntarily:

- take on new technical challenges
- seek out and respond to internal customer needs
- find ways to improve support systems and develop and refine administrative procedures
- deploy, utilize and network information to speed up delivery and productivity
- learn to be 'proactive' and to want to understand the rationale behind important management decisions which impact on their work.

The SMT cycle

The time it takes to develop a group of individuals into a properly performing SMT rather depends on the culture within which these teams are nurtured. At the very least, they can be produced in two years. This is extremely rare and only happens in organizations that score full marks on each factor as laid out in the feasibility checklist at the beginning of this chapter. The more common experience for achieving SMT capability ranges from three to five years. This is bound to get shorter as technology and particularly information technology progresses.

SMTs are not self-perpetuating. This is often misunderstood by management who assume that once a team reaches the phase of self management, it will continue to perform to the same degree of achievement *ad infinitum*. This is definitely untrue. Although managers become freer to focus on strategy, innovation, new business growth and development, they are obliged to regenerate and inspire the SMT to move on to the next challenge. This can be achieved by reinforcing the principles of *Kaizen* and continuous improvement. This is done by establishing forums for discussion and review, face-to-face meetings with clients or potential clients and the successful SMT. SMT members can be co-opted onto other SMTs whilst still retaining their old membership status. Part of the ongoing development of SMTs includes renewed training on all subjects including sessions on innovation and creative thinking.

The following graph provides some idea of the transition periods from phase one to phase five.

Figure 6.1   *The evolution of self-managing teams*

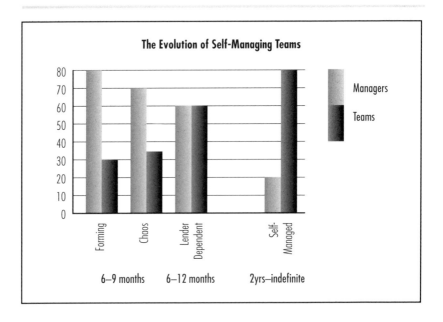

Rewarding the SMT

This topic can almost be developed into its own chapter. The rules of team reward are closely linked to the existing reward culture. This spans both the nature of the business (e.g. an IT company with a young dynamic workforce of materialistic executives as opposed to an organization with older, more conservative workers and work practices) and the accepted national norms of a particular country. For instance in Italy and many Latin countries, equality of reward is an important principle. You cannot reward one member of a team without rewarding everyone. This is completely contrary to the way most teams are rewarded in the individualistic work culture of the USA. In some organizations such as Dutton Engineering in the UK, the self-managing culture was so successfully introduced and implemented that teams began to set their own reward schemes, including having a say on levels of compensation.

The final sixth phase – change

There is one last phase, which has come in to disrupt the evolutionary process of SMTs. This is the phase of change – sometimes known as **reforming**. This is a typical response to modern economic conditions where Just-In-Time client driven necessity forces teams to regroup and in many cases disband. The effect on a team can be disastrous. Teams go into a state of mourning where the loss of loyal team players cannot be tolerated. New team players are added and are often treated with hostility and suspicion.

That is why successful organizations now try to introduce SMTs as part of a company-wide culture-change initiative. In many cases, the idea of developing SMTs on a one-off green field site basis can actually backfire because it may set a precedent that cannot be replicated anywhere else in the organization. This happened to a large chemical multinational organization in the USA. The company had to abandon the SMT project in their Kentucky plant, because it had become so successful that it had begun to raise expectations in other parts of the country which could not be fulfilled.

This is where the Japanese organization always scores highly in comparison with Western competitors. Japanese organizations build their cultures of empowerment and participation synchronously and simultaneously. Everyone is encouraged to think, act and speak the language of empowerment and *Kaizen* from the first day of joining the organization. This approach prevents the sixth phase of change from having any negative effects. The organization is built on a solid multi-skilled foundation of interdependent SMTs, which are linked together in a fluid matrix.

SUMMARY

In line with the philosophy of *Kaizen*, SMTs are part of a continuous process of evolutionary change. This change is brought about by economic, technological and social influences and affects every organization. Because of this constant paradigm shift, it is important for those who sponsor the move towards self management to be able to anticipate the future.

Not everyone will want to buy in at first. As Rosabeth Moss Kantor pointed out in her book *The Change Masters*:

Everything seems like failure in the middle.

Change managers and sponsors have got to expect resistance during the transition from conventional approaches to SMT working. They must also be able to answer the questions of those who are doubtful, suspicious or even afraid.

Shared knowledge and the dissemination of information is a key starting point when embarking on the long journey towards self management.

CHAPTER 7

Kaizen Teams are HOT –
Honest, Open and Trusting

BOB BRYANT

Associate, Europe Japan Centre

THE DRIVING FORCE BEHIND THIS chapter and behind the work I have done in introducing HOT relationships into organizations is the belief that it is the strength and quality of individual relationships that creates the synergy which produces exceptional team performance. This chapter shares some of my experience of working with HOT relationships, some of it in support of *Kaizen* initiatives. I do not pretend to have all the right answers because there is never a RIGHT answer to any issue. Your thoughts on the question are as valuable as mine, the only difference is that they originate from different experiences.

INTRODUCTION

I am making the assumption that having got this far in the book you are already a successful leader. Your success could be the anchor holding you back! We are all creatures of habit and we like to operate from our own comfort zones. Therefore, your decision making will be influenced by the constraints of your comfort zone.

As you read this chapter, I ask you to BELIEVE everything that you read. When you have finished it you can go back to your comfort zone if you wish. The little voice we all have in our heads will be questioning and criticizing new ideas and thoughts as they are developed; switch it off while you are reading and be open to the concepts in this chapter. When you have finished it ask yourself 'If this is the way things are, how would I have to change my behaviour and decision making to put these ideas into practice? How would I feel? What would I be saying and doing that is different?' In other words, try to identify any new insights or behaviour patterns that present themselves to you. Then try something new, take a risk and step outside your comfort zone.

WHY EFFECTIVE LEADERS SOMETIMES APPEAR COLD AND IMPERSONAL

HOT relationships provide the cement which bonds together the brilliance of individual performance to provide the benefit of exceptional team performance. Successful leaders are people who say it as it really is. They leave you with no doubt about what they think of your and others' performance. Sometimes this appears as unfeeling, hard or brutal. Leadership and team work is about knowing what you are all doing and then going for the same objective. Honest feedback ensures that this happens and while you may think that this is pretty obvious, it is amazing how few people grasp this precondition.

HOT relationships provide the cement which bonds together the brilliance of individual performance to provide the benefit of exceptional team performance.

Honest communication means that people know what you really think. Yet people can always find reasons for being flexible with the truth in their communication with others. This can range from 'sparing the feelings' of a close companion, maybe your partner's unflattering haircut for example, to a staff appraisal – 'I could not possibly tell him how badly he was performing, he would have been devastated'.

> *Write down a list of the excuses (remember they are not reasons) people use to justify being 'flexible with the truth' (or lying) when communicating with staff and with customers. The list will be long, the arguments familiar, and the reasons almost certainly spurious.*

Some reflection on the exercise and you will ruefully conclude that managers and staff regularly lie to each other under a number of guises:

> *I need to protect people's feelings . . .*
> *The staff would only worry if they knew the truth . . .*
> *He or she would have felt devalued if I had been totally honest . . .*

We will all have heard these phrases; we have all used them during the course of our work.

An evaluation I have conducted at a series of workshops under the title of *Who Tells Lies in the Workplace?* indicated that 100 per cent of the managers who participated considered that they were regularly lied to and that they had at some time or another lied to their colleagues and to their staff.

So how can we have effective communication if the parties involved believe people lie to them? Plainly we cannot, so instead people guess what is true, or, to use management terminology, 'we make assumptions'. All communications training programmes and skills development come to nought if at the end of the line, people are operating on estimates of the degree of truth and on guesswork. Very soon people's energy is deflected into protecting their backs, and the organization loses its creativity and risk-taking potential.

Case Study

A company managing director with whom I have worked had communicated bad news to a directly reporting manager, in effect reducing his status in the organization. The MD proudly described himself as having been caring in his communication (people often confuse caring with taking responsibility for the feelings of others) and was very pleased with himself.

When I then interviewed the manager, I found that the message he had received was completely different. He knew he was not performing well and had expected to be told. So oblique had been the feedback that he had heard an entirely misleading message and had in no way absorbed his effective demotion.

Working with the MD on straight communication was really based on getting him to step outside his comfort zone. With a lot of courage on his part, he told the manager the real situation in one short sentence. The end result was that the organization's performance improved because the problem had been dealt with.

The MD had grown because he had extended his comfort zone and found that the fear his imagination had created was not a reality. The manager was less stressed because he was at a level with which he could cope.

CREATING TRUST WITHIN AN ORGANIZATION

The way forward is to create a culture within the organization or team where communication is depersonalized and everyone knows that what is said is for the benefit of the team and the individuals within that team. It is not said to put someone down or belittle them.

To create such a culture one has first to have a vision of what behaviour in an honest culture would look like and feel like. One needs a conviction of the positive pay-off for the organization. It needs to be introduced into the organization in a way which enables it to grow because its benefit is in turn believed by all involved in the process.

Case Study

Cox Pharmaceuticals, a generic drug manufacturing company in Barnstaple, Devon decided it wanted to release the creative energy of everyone within their organization so they set about progressively changing their culture.

> *The company created a project leadership team. It was composed of a director and managers representing all the functions involved in the business: engineering, packing/dispatch, quality assurance, finance, personnel and training.*
>
> *The purpose of the project team was to show management's total support for the concept and to develop the company's vision of HOT (Honest, Open and Trusting) relationships. The project team was introduced to the foundation stones of HOT relationships and the concepts of Kaizen. The team developed their own culturally adapted version of HOT relationships. They then selected the packing and dispatch department in which to develop the new culture.*
>
> *The process of creating their own culture required some challenging discussion concerning the existing culture within the department. This took place within facilitated workshops using information on the department's view of its culture obtained by an interview process with staff.*

There is a case study of Cox Pharmaceuticals at the end of this chapter.

THE FIVE FOUNDATION STONES ON WHICH HOT RELATIONSHIPS ARE BUILT

A quick look at these foundation stones reveals that they are simple, well known and have been around for a long time. They are as follows.

1. Have a vision of what you are creating and share it.
2. Work for the success of the team.
3. Really listen to the other person.
4. Speak the truth clearly and honestly.
5. Acknowledge and appreciate the contribution of others.

One may well ask why, if these foundation stones are so transparently obvious, do we not use them in our day-to-day relationships. In my own case I know that the strength of my comfort zone leads me to being fearful of the consequences of being honest with people.

> *Before we handle each of these foundation stones in greater depth, take a moment to try to identify your own personal reason for being flexible with the truth (dishonest) and not being totally honest at work.*

1. Have a vision of what you are creating and share it

We talk of a company vision or strategic direction and sometimes a department vision which fits into the company strategic direction. However, we rarely talk of individual and personal visions of the future we want to create. If you are going on holiday the first thing that is created is your vision of the holiday you want. Usually you share your vision with all the people who will be affected by it, most commonly the rest of the family. As time goes by the vision is modified by the feedback others offer and what emerges is the vision which is shared and meets everyone's needs.

The skill of a modern manager is to use all the foundation stones of HOT relationships to produce a situation where the vision of what success looks and feels like is shared among colleagues and supports the broader strategy of the company.

Planning, designing, and ultimately enjoying your holiday is a process of successive refinement and development of what everyone wants. Most people use visualization to a high degree in the process – they build a vision.

Imagine the effect on your attitude and enjoyment of work if you and your colleagues developed a shared vision of the future and were working towards achieving it. Unfortunately it rarely happens. Managers sometimes believe that anarchy would result if everybody had their own vision of the future. This is a possible outcome, so the skill of a modern manager is to use all the foundation stones of HOT relationships to produce a situation where the vision of what success looks and feels like is shared among colleagues and supports the broader strategy of the company.

People often pose the question of what happens if their vision of the future is incompatible with that of the organization. The only honest answer is to resign and find an employer whose vision is compatible with your own. If you do not act, eventually your employer will see your lack of support for the company vision and take the appropriate action.

> *Think about your own personal vision of the future at work. Then identify three reasons why you will not share it with your colleagues.*

2. Work for the success of the team

This is our second foundation stone; first some context. We develop in a very competitive society and promotion is believed to be won as the result of our individual performance. This leads to behaviour patterns where we make decisions based upon what is good for us as individuals. The high fliers in leadership, however, appear to be those who can create exceptional teams. The evidence is that the exceptional team is created by the players working for each other's success. No clearer example can be found than in the field of team sports like football or rugby.

Imagine a workplace where everybody is placing the interest of their colleagues before their own concerns. No more passing the buck, no more refusal to involve yourself in the concerns of others. This open-handedness with your own time and energy matched similarly with the expectation that help will be freely and willingly provided for you if needed or asked for. This is the climate of the high performing team.

3. Really listen to the other person

Listening is something we do automatically and we all think we are efficient and effective listeners. We rarely try to measure the effectiveness of our listening skills. We do not ask subordinates their opinion of our listening skills. Do you find that you listen more intently to your manager than you do to your staff? Have you been on a listening training programme?

> *As an exercise, form a judgement of the effectiveness of your listening skills by seeking feedback from others. Discussing the subject with others, particularly your partner and your children if you have any, will be revealing.*

In many organizations an 'interrupt' culture exists. This usually implies a senior person interrupting junior staff because he or she, consciously or subconsciously, considers their point of view to be more

---

Case Study

At Cox Pharmaceuticals one of the HOT relationship teams had completed its week's work ahead of schedule. So the team which was composed of operatives and maintenance engineers offered their services to support the work of the other teams in the department.

In another example, one of the operatives took on forklift truck work (with proper training) so that the forklift truck driver could achieve his personal ambition of being trained to carry out mechanical maintenance on the line. At their team meetings the prevailing theme was 'What can I do for you?'

---

important than the other person's. Sometimes the interruption comes because of the person's enthusiasm to put their point of view over.

It was not until I had left my role as a Chief Executive and become a business coach that I found out about my personal listening skills. They were terrible. I was an interrupter. My staff would be half-way through telling me about a problem and I would be interrupting with the solution and getting on with the next problem. Then Charles Smith from America introduced me to the Indian Talking Stick. This is a stick that American Indians placed in the centre of the tent when they were having a tribal conference. The person who wanted to speak would pick up the stick and while they were talking no one could interrupt, ask questions, make comments or disbelieve what was being said. The person holding the stick was tribal chief until he relinquished it.

I tried the talking stick with a group of people I used to work with. The rules we applied were simple: no interruptions, no questions and no comments until after the meeting was over.

Subsequently we analyzed the experience. The people involved believed that they had achieved four hours' worth of communication in a single hour. They felt that not having to worry about answering questions enabled them to concentrate on the message they were trying to get over. Knowing there were not going to be any clever remarks to put them down meant they did not have to be ready to defend themselves. No interruptions meant that they actually said what they had to say.

As far as the listeners were concerned they really listened to the WHOLE statement rather than switching off while they thought of something to say.

A really powerful means for improving listening technique is to hold a listening meeting. This is particularly effective if you are in a dispute with someone. Both parties agree to hold two meetings for a specified duration (start with ten or fifteen minutes). At the first meeting, person A speaks to person B. Person B is not allowed to do anything other than listen, no comments at all. At the end of the meeting the two parties go their separate ways with no discussion about what was said. The second meeting is held later, at least three hours after the first one. This time person B does the talking and person A the listening. Again no interruption and no discussion after the meeting. The discussion of the experience and communication from the listening meeting takes place later, at least 24 hours after the second meeting.

A really powerful means for improving listening technique is to hold a listening meeting.

> *Identify someone with whom you cannot reach agreement or with whom you are having a difficult relationship. Invite them to participate in a listening meeting. Be sure you identify the ground rules described above and stick to them.*

4. Speak the truth clearly and honestly

We talked earlier in this chapter about being honest in communication and not being flexible with the truth. This applies not only to the content of a problem but to the interpersonal relationships of people involved in a communication. There is no reason why you should feel intimidated by a discussion with a superior. Using position power, as it is sometimes called, is simply managerial jargon for being a bully. One of the strengths of HOT relationships is that it allows humaneness to be an accepted part of the workplace culture. This results in our strengths being appreciated and our weaknesses accepted.

A word of warning; being honest and 'saying it as it is' does not mean being disrespectful of the feelings of others. Calling a spade a spade, as the saying goes, sometimes covers an insensitivity to others that can border on bullying.

You will know you are not in that category when your motivation is the other person's success. Another check is to be truthful to yourself about whether you are secretly gloating about being 'honest'. If you are, then you are potentially in bullying mode.

Case Study

In Britain's National Health Service, surgeons can be temperamental and this leads to some aggressive behaviour. I knew a senior theatre nurse who was always calm and polite; sometimes I thought she emanated an almost saintly aura. No one ever stepped out of line in her presence, be they a senior manager or irascible surgeon. When I asked her why this was, she was surprised. She had never thought of it. She had always assumed she would be treated with respect and so she was. This kind of expectation is subtly but accurately communicated in behaviour and engenders reciprocity of expectation in any dialogue.

---

5. Acknowledge and appreciate the contribution of others

We all enjoy being recognized and we appreciate being acknowledged, praised or thanked. You could call it stroking. Often we are too embarrassed to accept praise or to bestow it on other people. In addition to praise this foundation stone speaks to the need for gratitude, being thankful for the contribution of others. Admitting our need for help and acknowledging it when somebody has saved our bacon, or deployed their special skills and knowledge on our behalf strengthens relationships.

This is a very good point in the chapter for me to make my own personal acknowledgement and appreciation of the influence of the work of Maggie and Tony Turnbull and their colleagues in The McLane Group. Maggie influenced my thinking and introduced me to high performance coaching by taking me out of my personal comfort zone with honest feedback. My success to date is a direct result of her efforts and those of Steve Radcliffe.

Identify any people in your workplace that you do not get on with or whom you deliberately avoid. Assume that you are the cause of these feelings. Identify how you could behave which would cause an improvement. Then go and actually develop a better relationship with two of those colleagues.

Case Study

A Managing Director with whom I have worked made a point of both openly admitting his mistakes, and his lack of knowledge on some issues. He coupled this frankness with the apparent ability to recognize and be able to name each individual in this 1000 employee organization.

In truth he achieved this feat of memory by careful research before he walked through a department. No matter how he did it, his openness and recognition meant that he was trusted and, as a result, given information which would not normally have been shared with him.

MANAGING THE FEAR WITHIN US

Everyone has fear and it is our response to fear which in large measure controls our behaviour. In the business world our fear ranges from losing our job, looking a fool in front of the others, not being in control of our staff, not knowing what to do, and even wanting to hide.

How can we manage fear? An examination of the approach used by stuntmen is worthy of consideration.

From the experience of stunt people we can devise some simple rules for managing our own fear; here is a four part process.

1. Be honest with yourself and define exactly what it is you are frightened of; it helps to write it down or draw it.
2. Talk openly about your fears and open yourself up to listen to other people's comments.
3. Break your fear down into its component parts and identify an action you can take to minimize the consequence of each part of the fear.
4. Finally, act upon your instincts and move forward.

A manager I was coaching was so fearful of losing his job that he was taking no risks and making no decisions. This, of course, increased the likelihood that he would lose his job. So we worked together using these simple tools. He defined his fear as being twofold: first he thought his director had no faith in him and second, he would be in financial difficulties if he was sacked.

Case Study

Like you and me, stuntmen and women have fears and they cannot simply pretend they are not there. So a culture has developed of openly talking about their fears with other stunt people, and with the stunt co-ordinator, usually an experienced stunt person who is assigned to each film. Among their tasks, stunt co-ordinators are there to encourage openness about all of the problems a stunt may create. Each and every fear is broken down into its many and separate parts and solutions to each issue identified and agreed before moving on. The stunt person does not blindly accept that it will be all right on the day. Concerns are openly discussed with everyone and the experienced stunt people make their thoughts known but do not degrade the fear of the performer. At the end of this process there always remains an element of the unknown. This represents say, 10 per cent of the total stunt – it is the professional risk.

Our next step was to talk openly about his fears and in doing so test whether his fears had a basis in reality. The process revealed that the future was not so bleak even if he did lose his job. He calculated what he would receive if they sacked him and how long he could survive with his financial resources.

Next he decided to act upon his instincts and he discussed with his boss his fears and perceptions of his performance.

The end result was that his fear disappeared as he took control of his working performance.

Take an issue about which you are fearful and work through the above four rules for managing fear. With regard to talking openly about your fears you may wish, in the first instance, to use someone you really trust. But later try it in your workplace and evaluate the reaction.

USE OF QUESTIONS WITHIN HOT RELATIONSHIPS

The concept of HOT relationships within an organization implies an environment in which everyone works together with total trust. A major element of such a culture is how questions are used.

The concept of HOT relationships within an organization implies an environment in which everyone works together with total trust.

Questions can be used to build or destroy. Look at the comparative examples below which help delineate the power, positive and negative, which can be exercised through questioning.

To demonstrate your power over people.

or

To make people feel secure enough to say what they feel.

To demonstrate you know more than other people do.

or

To let people show how much they know.

To identify who is to blame or who got it wrong.

or

To identify the need to find answers to a problem.

To prove somebody is wrong.

or

To say I want to help you however I can.

Often an organization's culture will claim to be open, to encourage participation and to welcome input. The behaviour of senior people within that culture will greatly affect what actually happens, rather than what purports to be the case.

> *To investigate how you tend to use questions, identify examples in your own environment that fall into the categories described by the above examples. Then plan how you might use questions at your next meeting to help develop HOT relationship with the participants. At this meeting try listening not telling.*

Case Study

A Director with whom I have worked complained vigorously that his direct subordinates did not produce any creative suggestions in meetings or take the initiative. Probing a bit deeper I found that the director had been with the company for some 20 years, was a world expert on his subject, worked 15 hour days and could even be contacted by mobile phone when on holiday.

As if his formidable credentials were not enough, he was an expert in destroying people's position with the short sharp question.

It was of course no surprise that his department was in effect a one man band and would continue to be so, for to offer suggestions was to invite being cut down to size by the demolishing question.

PROBLEM SOLVING IN A HOT ENVIRONMENT

The pressure for instant solutions to problems in busy and pressured working environments often leads to short-term thinking so that the cause of the problem is never really dealt with. *Kaizen* stresses the need for root cause analysis, and in a HOT relationships team, the following creative problem-solving action plan might help you to aim for long-term problem solving.

1. What solution to the problem will contribute most to achieving your vision?
2. How can your team create that solution?
3. What questions can you ask that will clarify the problems and identify the components of the solution?
4. How can you change your behaviour to produce the ideal solution?
5. What stops you changing your behaviour?
6. What actions can you take which are different from your past behaviour?
7. Do not allow the problem to obscure the vision.
8. Then return to 1. and start again.

The following quote from German philosopher, Arthur Schopenhauer, may help:

> *The Truth evolves through three steps: firstly it is ridiculed, secondly it is violently opposed and finally it is accepted as self-evident.*

A CASE STUDY OF THE BENEFITS OF HOT RELATIONSHIPS

Deciding to introduce HOT relationships

Cox Pharmaceuticals, a successful generic drugs manufacturer, introduced their version of HOT relationships into the packing and dispatch department. The project started in 1995 when the company, despite being successful, was looking at ways to stretch their culture and their performance. They reviewed various forms of cultural change that were available: self managing teams; pure *Kaizen*; extending TQM; and *Kaizen* supported by HOT relationships.

After an in-depth evaluation of the various alternatives from a number of management consultants, they selected the Europe Japan Centre's *Kaizen* with HOT relationships for three reasons:

1. The process of introducing the culture would be organized by the Europe Japan Centre's (EJC's) Business Coaching Team (Bob Bryant and Pat Wellington).

2. One of the fundamentals of the coaching concept was that Cox would be presented with a range of ideas and then supported in creating their own vision of HOT relationships.

3. HOT relationships would build upon the Cox philosophy of *really* valuing the company staff.

Stage 1: management commitment

To ensure there was visible support for the concept a management project team was created. The team was to provide leadership, ensure visibility of support for the pilot teams and, where appropriate, ensure that the old culture did not block progress.

Stage 2: creating Cox's version of HOT relationships

A cultural needs analysis of the existing Cox culture within the packaging and despatch department was undertaken. Bob Bryant and Pat Wellington interviewed a cross-section of staff who had volunteered to be involved in the project. There was no management restriction on the type of questions and information that could be collected.

A report was then prepared which defined the Cox culture within the department from the view point of the shop floor staff and from management's perspective. This enabled the gap between the existing environment and the vision of a company with HOT relationships to be defined. From EJC's viewpoint this identified the size of the hill we were going to be climbing in partnership with Cox.

A series of meetings was organized so that the volunteers, middle management and senior management could be introduced to *Kaizen* and to HOT relationships. The finance and technical directors participated in these meetings, on an equal footing with everyone else. Everyone had been informed that the objective of the meetings was two-way communication. Bob Bryant and Pat Wellington informed them of the possibilities arising from *Kaizen* and HOT relationships. The Cox team identified what the new culture would look like for them.

At the end of this phase of the programme a document was produced which defined the principles of HOT relationships that Cox intended to develop in the packing and despatch department. A series of meetings was organized for a group of staff who had volunteered to be involved in the project. They were introduced to the philosophy so that they could make a reasoned choice as to whether they wished to continue to be involved in the project.

Providing the pilot team with the hard and soft skills for the new culture

The concept of HOT relationships is about people trusting each other. Being given the freedom, within clear guidelines, to organize their work and make decisions. To be seen as equals with a valuable contribution to make to the decision-making process, listening and believing the information people outside their function provide them with. So often organizations make the mistake of assuming the shop floor staff need only to know about the new idea because they have the skills to do the rest. The factor that made the Cox programme such a success was that Cox did not make this mistake. The company decided to assume a no-knowledge base for everyone and ran a series of workshops on communication, decision making, problem solving and team working in the context of the new HOT relationship principles. These workshops brought together managers, supervisors, engineers and operatives who developed their new culture together.

Letting the new teams loose

The management then created the first two teams and let them loose, figuratively speaking, to go forward and learn by their mistakes. At all times senior management and the EJC coaches were in the background to provide support if the going got really rough. As is always the case when you trust people, they exceed your expectations. Because the teams set their own objectives they were not limited to the expectations of senior management. For example, a specific team's objective was zero machine down time. Whereas an experienced manager may have gone for a 5 or 10 per cent improvement in this performance criterion, the team was also looking for 50 per cent improvement in productivity. All of the targets the teams set themselves were stretching the boundaries.

The benefits to Cox from introducing a new culture

The benefits were many and varied; the following list provides some examples.

- Reduction in the number of middle level management by the removal of the grade of supervisor and deputy supervisor.
- Productivity improvement which averaged, after six months, 32 per cent but had, with some products, gone as high as 200 per cent.
- Removal of the 'them and us' relationship between managers, engineers and operatives.
- Introduction of shop floor pressure on management to introduce changes that at first sight appeared to have no production benefit. Examples of this type of change are installing a telephone line for outside calls; computer terminal for the operatives to examine management performance data; overtime being identified and approved

by the team; a room for the team to leave the production line for meetings as and when they chose; the team to receive production requirements as soon as the production controller received them from sales engineers, and operatives being able to discuss issues with suppliers without seeking management approval.

- Staff took the initiative to do things differently. Operatives used their relationship with warehouse staff to find out what stock was on hand. This enabled them to prepare for sudden requests from customers which could not be met by stock.
- Gossip between team members in the restaurant became positive.
- Shared training experience increased the rate of learning new skills.
- Team members had higher expectations in terms of team performance than the managers.

The success of the project, which has led to Cox rolling the concept out to more teams, was because managers took the step of trusting their staff. The staff responded to the trust with enthusiasm as can be seen by the following quotes from the team's first quarterly report:

The team was full of enthusiasm and eager to get to grips with the two new lines. Immediately we hit our first hurdle, we had only one line ready to run. This was our first taste of 'It's our problem, it's up to us to sort it out'. So we did. One week later the second machine was running with tooling made in house by Keith.

In the following weeks many such hurdles have presented themselves and as a team we have overcome them.

There have been major benefits in areas breaking down barriers by dealing with people who can help us resolve our problems.

The enthusiasm is still with us and the sky is really the limit. The encouragement and support given from all areas will help us achieve our goals.

A change in working relationships is never a simple rite of passage. However, as I write this text, the original teams we worked with are still in place, and they discuss, challenge, develop and grow. More teams with the same values are being created. There is a sense of commitment within the teams that is contagious, and as a Centre we feel privileged to be working with them on their voyage of discovery.

SUMMARY

It is a prerequisite of high performance in teams that they operate in an atmosphere of mutual trust. Trust is only established when each member of the team believes that all others are behaving with honesty and integrity and working for the team's success. Good listening skills and good feedback skills, and acknowledging the contribution of others, help to generate HOT relationships in the team and so contribute to team effectiveness.

PART THREE

Dealing with Problems

CHAPTER 8

Changing the Game – Re-directing Kaizen Teams

JOHN HALL

Associate, Europe Japan Centre

IN SPITE OF ALL GOOD intentions, much team training and organizational preparedness, teams still run into trouble. Causes can be within the team, or external to it, or there could be a change in alignment between the team and the organization.

John Hall introduces a fresh approach, involving focusing techniques, energy, and a particular use of organizational questions that will get your team (and your organization) back on track.

INTRODUCTION

Thinking about teams that you know, ask yourself when you are likely to notice if they need re-directing.

Sometimes it's obvious. For instance, the team could disintegrate into individuals all complaining about the intransigence of each other, or the team misses an important delivery date. Sometimes it is less obvious. For instance, the team ceases to communicate as much as it may have done before.

Much has already been written about team failure and how to recognize the symptoms of imminent collapse and what ingredients are necessary to prevent this. The purpose of this chapter is not to repeat those things that have been written about elsewhere. Instead, the aim is to look specifically at team direction and re-direction and introduce a technique that can energize or re-energize teams in a positive direction.

DIRECTION AND ENERGY

Notice that I am connecting the words direction and energy. There can be a strong connection between them and both will exist in a team that is really going places. However, there can be direction and no energy, or even energy and no direction. What one needs is energy in the right direction. This link between energy and direction and the consequences of it can be summarized as in Table 8.1 below.

Even this simple model can give us some insights into when teams need re-direction. A low energy/low direction team needs direction as does the high energy/low direction team. These teams are likely to run into trouble.

A more interesting area is the high sense of direction and low

Table 8.1 *The link between a team's energy and direction*

Team's sense of direction	Team's energy	
	High	Low
High	Team likely to succeed	Team likely to produce poor results
Low	Team likely to go off at a tangent or become frustrated	Team likely to wither

energy box. It raises the question as to why a team, given good direction, would have low energy. There could be several answers which might include insufficient resources, internal team problems, unrealistic beliefs about team potential, no perceivable benefits to team members, or the team may not believe that the direction is the right one.

Whatever the reason, before we decide to re-direct a team either from the inside or the outside, we have to find out whether the team itself feels it has a strong SENSE of direction. The organization may feel there is strong direction, but the team may feel otherwise. Sensing the team's view is the first step. Is the team clear on what to do and the reason why it has been asked to do it?

If the strength of direction is there, the team should be able to say what is important about its future work, how that work will help the organization move forward and why it is essential that time and effort go into the activity. Although organizations may have convinced themselves that they have set teams up in precisely this way, the reality is what is believed within the team, and that is what needs testing. If you find any hesitation then you know something must be done. That something may have to be at both the organization and team level.

I have noticed that many organizations can have business plans but may experience difficulties in showing how the various strategies and change projects fit together. At team or departmental level terms of reference or objectives may not be well connected.

Such connections are important to enable *Kaizen* teams to have a motivational appreciation of the importance of their work. For a *Kaizen* team to move forward, its direction must be aligned with the organization's direction. Ask yourself what might happen if the team has:

For a Kaizen team to move forward, its direction must be aligned with the organization's direction.

- only a weak sense of direction; or
- a strong sense of direction that is aligned with the company; or
- a strong sense of direction that is NOT aligned.

In the table below, each of the above is related to both weak and strong organization direction and the consequences given.

Table 8.2 *The alignment of team and organization direction*

Team's sense of direction	Organization direction	
	Weak	Strong
Weak	Team likely to wither	Team likely to lack commitment
Strong but not aligned with organization	Team likely to generate resistance	Team likely to clash with others
Strong and aligned with organization	Team likely to produce results	Team likely to produce results

Again a simple diagram can produce insights. Boxes 1 and 2 at the top of the table clearly suggest a team in need of re-direction. The middle two boxes (3 and 4) dealing with non-aligned teams also suggest difficulty.

A strong non-aligned team pushing forward in a weakly directed organization (Box 3) is likely to bring forward complaints about it being pushy and arrogant, about causing trouble and having no sense of what the managers believe is important. This is not inevitable, just likely.

A strong non-aligned team pushing forward in a strongly directed organization (Box 4) will soon attract criticism of disruption and wasting resources. These teams certainly need re-directing and some review, as first appearances would suggest the team does not know what is going on, or someone connected with the team does not agree with the overall direction.

Boxes 5 and 6 at the bottom of the table should both produce results, although a strong team pushing forward along a weak direction might also be accused of being too pushy.

Listening out for clues about how other people see a team might give you an insight into difficulties between company direction and team direction. If you hear criticism of pushiness, or arrogance or lack of commitment then you know you have to do something . . . but what?

If action is required then it could fall into two categories – gentle coaching or stronger re-direction.

If the team is broadly doing the right thing, yet there are complaints, then the team needs some gentle coaching on its responsibility to create positive perceptions of what it does. This can be done quite easily with a facilitator hosting a team review session. The facilitator would help the team review what sort of perceptions it is creating and what it is seeking to create. Interestingly, teams may focus on customers and be concerned about how a negative action might impact on them. They may not however look at how to create positive customer perceptions in the first place. They may also not think of seeking to influence the perceptions of peer teams or other people who can influence the team's perception. This in effect is all about internal marketing – a very useful skill for all teams, no matter who they are. It often generates a fair degree of interest to ask a team to talk about the fourth law of marketing as proposed by Al Ries and James Trout.[1] This simply says that marketing is about a battle of perceptions and not a battle of products. Can the perception of a team be more important than the work it does?

If re-direction is required, then the technique of mapping that follows will help. First I will introduce the underlying principles, then the technique itself and finally examine its practical implementation.

THE ENABLING LAWS

Every practical technique is based on some underlying principles, assumptions or laws. *Kaizen* is based on a set of principles. In business there is a tendency to interchange words like principle and laws, so with that in mind, here are the enabling laws for an organization.

The first law

'Every organization enables its customers to achieve something.'

This law is important in that it gets an organization to be clear on what value it provides to the customer. It goes beyond just responding to customer needs. It seeks to ascertain what the product or service will **do** for the customer. It demands that you think beyond 'woolly' expressions such as lower costs or increased profits or productivity and find out what practically and tangibly you will enable each customer to do.

This will highlight the importance of the product or service to the customer and also enable you to reflect back within the organization how important the work of your organization is.

This first enabling law builds upon the first *Kaizen* principle – focus on customers.

The second law

'In an organization with good direction, every activity enables the mission.'

This law simply requires activities to be linked to the mission. In an organization operating management by objectives, you simply break the objectives down until you get down to the task level. Every task or activity should then connect back to the mission. If an activity cannot connect back to the mission then it should be challenged as to whether it is a wasteful activity.

In practice, this process does not happen except in the more sophisticated organization. If the process does exist, it tends to be very detailed and not good at handling large amounts of change. To make matters more difficult, organizations have different interpretations as to what constitutes a mission and whether this is measurable. However, the logic is sound. If there is a measurable mission all activity within the organization should enable it. If you break the second law, then you will have wasteful activity on your hands – something which *Kaizen* seeks to eliminate.

The third law

'In an organization with good direction, every individual enables some other individual.'

This is almost the human equivalent of the second law – but not quite. The logic is to keep in mind that everyone has customers within the organization and that they are real people. Notice the similarity to the first law – just as the organization enables its customers, every individual in the organization enables others within the organization. In a similar way, teams will also enable people.

The fourth law

'Organizations make better progress if they minimize internal disabling activities.'

The trick, of course, is to identify what they are and then have the courage to do something about them. All change can potentially cause disabling activities, as can last-minute panics. The continuous improvement philosophy behind Kaizen leads to smoother transitions and constant organizational learning and this represents a practical approach to following the fourth law.

USING THE LAWS:
THE TECHNIQUE OF MAPPING

There are other laws of enablement. (One other law relates to a Kaizen principle – 'To better enable your customers, you have to better enable your employees'.)

It is the first four, though, that concern us as a basis for the technique for re-directing a team.

By applying the laws, we can not only establish whether there is good direction, we can also challenge some business strategies. For instance, if your organization has signed up for gaining a good practice award or a charter mark, what is that going to enable your organization to do?

If we can make use of the laws and find a more straightforward way to link all the activities in your organization together so you could see how everything fitted – and what did not – would that be useful? And if we could do it in such a participative way that teams could relate their direction to the overall direction of the organization, would that help your teams go forward?

We can do all the above things by producing a map of connections that is not only simple and easy to communicate, but will also show who enables whom, and what enables what, and potentially highlight some waste activity.

A map of questions

This will not be a map of objectives. Objectives tend to be very specific and less likely to inspire. Instead this will be a map of **questions.** These will not be just any questions. They are a particular type of questions.

Each question has a common structure – a structure you may well recognize. The questions are in the form of challenges and each one looks something like this:

'How can we (or I) . . . do . . . something?'

The 'How . . .' is designed to elicit a practical route to achieving the rest of the sentence.

The '. . . we . . .' is designed to ensure that someone has ownership for the challenge.

The '. . . do . . .' can be replaced by any action verb that suits the occasion. We could use, for example, 'achieve', 'make', 'reduce', 'increase', 'lower', 'influence', 'help'.

The '. . . something' can be replaced by anything that is easy to understand in concrete terms. By concrete terms, I mean you should be able to describe the outcome of the challenge either as if it existed, or as a precise quantity.

The SCOPE test

To check whether any challenge you have is in an appropriate form, you should use the SCOPE test where:

S = Singular
C = Challenging
O = Ownership
P = Positive
E = Easy to understand.

The **S** for singular means we only deal with ONE challenge at a time. In practice, any challenge containing two verbs linked by an 'and' will not pass the singular test. A challenge that reads 'How can we develop and maintain our infrastructure?' is two different challenges.

The **C** for challenging means only challenges that indicate a significant and challenging difference to the existing situation should go on your map. Any challenge that is trivial should not be there. It is up to the team putting the map together to decide what is, and what is not, trivial. If you fill your map with trivial things you will not see what is important.

The **O** for ownership means that if a sentence has not got 'we', or an 'I' in it, it will fail the O test. If you do not own the challenge, it should not be on your organization's (or team's map).

The **P** for positive is meant in two senses. First, it should be a statement of what you will do and not what you will not do. Second, it is about being positive about people. 'How can we stop X from ruining this situation?' is not a positive challenge. 'How can we ensure X understands the task?' is far more positive.

The **E** stands for easy to understand in concrete terms. The aim of this test is to eliminate vague challenges such as 'How can we empower our people?' It may sound a good challenge but what does it mean in practice? Much management jargon is vague, so anything of a jargon nature should be eliminated.

> *It is worth pausing for a moment to test your new knowledge on the challenges below and to determine whether they pass the SCOPE test. Apply the SCOPE test to the following questions.*
>
> 1. *How can we reduce costs and put up sales?*
>
> 2. *How can we become more customer focused?*
>
> 3. *How can we prevent marketing messing it up again?*
>
> 4. *How can our customers better understand our products?*
>
> 5. *How can we move the office furniture?*

In the first example you may have noticed the 'and' between the two verbs. There are two separate challenges here – 'How can we reduce costs? and 'How can we put up sales?'. The challenge as written fails the singular test.

The second challenge is interesting. Everyone can nod their heads in agreement that becoming more customer focused sounds good and is a fine principle, but what are we agreeing to that is practical? What does customer focus actually mean? Unless the team that put this challenge together have a very practical and common understanding about what they are specifically talking about, then this challenge fails the 'easy to understand in concrete terms' part of the SCOPE test.

The third challenge is not about being positive and respectful and fails the positive test. It also could fail the 'easy to understand in concrete terms' test as there is no clear definition of what the 'it' refers to. A challenge starting 'How can we influence marketing to . . .?' would be better.

The fourth challenge fails the ownership test. There is no '*we*' in it, there is no 'I' in it. It would be far better expressed as 'How can we help our customers better understand our products?'. This puts the challenge back into our control.

The fifth challenge is not very challenging for most teams. It probably is for the local removals company though! However, if it is not challenging for the local executive team, it should not go on the team's map. It therefore would fail the 'C' test of SCOPE.

FINDING YOUR OWN CHALLENGES

Every objective you have, every problem you have, and every activity you do is a challenge in disguise. Here are some examples of objectives and purposes turning into challenges.

- If your objective is to produce so many thousands of a product this year, your challenge becomes 'How can we produce so many thousands of this product this year?'
- If your problem is making a bottle top go on straight in a production line, your challenge becomes 'How can I ensure the bottle top goes on straight?'

With activities you need to do a bit more work.

Every objective you have, every problem you have, and every activity you do is a challenge in disguise.

For example, if you are responsible for the credit control section, ask yourself what is the purpose of the activity. If the purpose of the activity is to get the due money in by the due date then the challenge becomes 'How can we ensure we get the due money in by the due date?' So one way of turning an activity into a challenge is to ask about the purpose of the activity.

Another way to turn an activity into a challenge is to think of the results of the activity. Imagine your activity is loading lorries. As you may have been trained to do this in a certain way, then your challenge is 'How can I ensure that lorries are loaded in the right way?' The answer may be known, and this challenge may not be challenging enough for your map, but the reason for using it here is to show how an activity can be made into a challenge. As you will learn below, even a pretty small challenge can be the starting point for progressing towards a mission.

Linking the challenges with the organization's mission

Now that you can both handle the challenges and identify some, we need to connect them. For this we call on the second enabling law. If every activity enables the mission, and every activity presents a challenge, then it would seem reasonable that we can connect every challenge to a challenge about the mission. This is exactly the case. To do it we simply ask a question that will take us towards the mission.

That question is:

'If we could achieve (this), what does that enable us to do?'

We treat the answer to this challenge as another possible challenge.

Going back to our lorry example, our question would be 'If we got all the lorries loaded in the right way, what would that enable us to do?' With this example, you would certainly be likely to get some interesting responses! They might include 'It would enable us to keep damage in transit down to zero', 'It would enable us to have a longer tea break', 'It would enable us to get the vehicles away faster'.

If we took a serious response such as 'It would enable us to keep damage in transit to zero', the challenge then is 'How can we keep damage in transit to zero?' We have thus turned the answer into another challenge.

We can ask the upwards question again – 'If we could keep damage in transit to zero, what would this enable us to do?'

The response could be 'It would enable us to reduce customer complaints'. So the next challenge becomes 'How can we reduce customer complaints?' If you applied the upwards question yet again you might get 'It would enable us to get more customer re-orders'. So a higher level challenge becomes 'How can we get more customer re-orders?'

You have probably noticed that we now have a hierarchy of challenges as below:

Figure 8.3

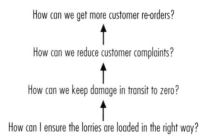

Notice that the bigger challenges go on top and the arrows point to the bigger challenges. This is the format we use for mapping. Notice too that a 'How can I . . .' challenge is linked to a 'How can we . . .' challenge.

This approach allows an individual or team to connect their

challenges to organizational challenges. If the organizational challenge cannot be found there is work to be done!

Going downwards on your map

To go downwards, we apply another short question to a challenge. This is:

'What are the issues?'

The question may be short, but it is not simple. Ask yourself what the word 'issue' means. You may have a clear definition, but many people find it has ambiguity. This ambiguity is deliberate. The intention is to generate a wide range of responses from a team and a slightly ambiguous question helps to do this. Fortunately the question, even though ambiguous, is well enough understood so requests for clarification are unusual.

As the most important issues come out, the team turns them into challenges.

Let's look at an example. If the starting challenge was 'How can we have more time to make the products?' we would respond to this by

Figure 8.4

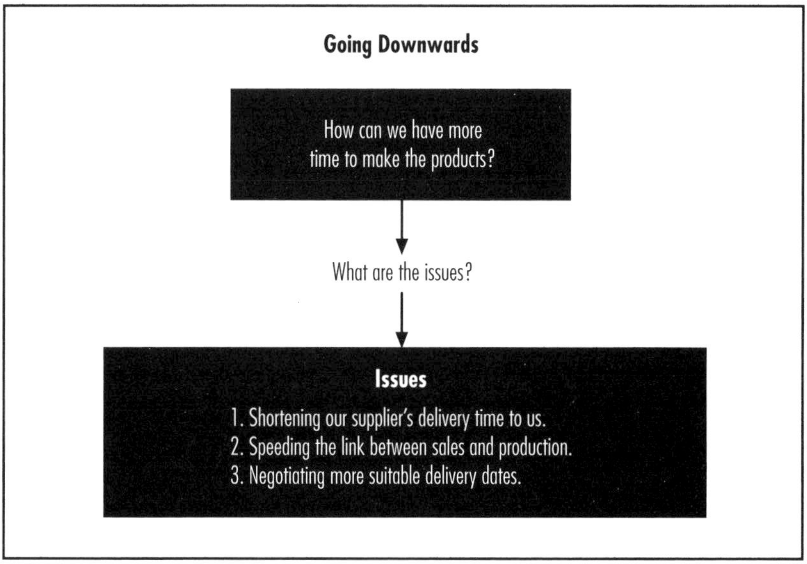

Going Downwards

How can we have more
time to make the products?

What are the issues?

Issues

1. Shortening our supplier's delivery time to us.
2. Speeding the link between sales and production.
3. Negotiating more suitable delivery dates.

asking the question 'What are the main issues involved in having more time to make our products?'

It is likely you can think of several issues. Let's pretend that the issues are:

1. shortening our supplier's delivery time to us
2. speeding the link between sales and production; and
3. negotiating more suitable delivery dates.

These issues are simply turned into challenges by introducing the expression 'How can we' in front of them, e.g. 'How can we shorten our supplier's delivery time to us?', 'How can we speed the link between production and sales?', 'How can we negotiate more suitable delivery dates?'.

Now we know the lower challenges we can start forming the map as below.

Figure 8.5

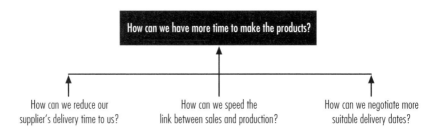

We can ask the downwards questions again and go down further. If we were to do that, we would be breaking down big issues into smaller and smaller issues, until we got to one that was too trivial to discuss further (and so falls off the bottom of the map) or one that is difficult and needs a problem-solving process. Going downwards effectively takes us into problem solving, whereas going upwards takes us towards strategy.

USING A MAPPING AID

We can now design a simple mapping aid, incorporating all we have learnt so far, as follows.

Figure 8.6

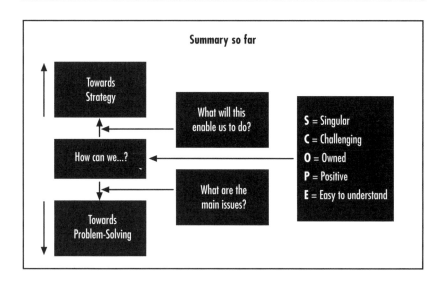

With this mapping aid, you can construct some basic maps. Your starting point will depend on how much clarity is already in your organization, department or team. If you already have a good organization, department or team mission, you should work down from there. If you have not, start by identifying a major challenge for the team, then work upwards until you reach a mission for the team (and one that connects into the rest of the organization!). Then work downwards from there.

If you want to have a go at mapping your own responsibilities, there are two other rules that may be useful to you. They are as follows.

1. Every challenge can only go upwards to one other challenge. However many things you discover that a particular challenge would enable you to do, you pick just one of them – the most important one. This will keep you pretty focused.

2. Every challenge can only give rise to a maximum of five issues. This will limit you in some cases to deciding what is really important. However, in practice, you will find that each challenge gives rise to two or three major issues.

These rules and what you have learned so far will allow you to experiment with the basic method. There are a number of additional tricks of the trade and additional upwards and downwards questions which will help you strengthen your map and resolve mapping difficulties, particularly when you apply it with teams. Not everyone in a team thinks the same and mapping with a team will get people involved, create sharing, bring out differences and help resolve them. The basic method will still do a lot for you as it will clarify your thinking and you may find the linking method useful in your presentations.

To produce good maps though you should do it with a team and use a facilitator. The facilitator will look after the process, get you out of the frequent *non sequiturs* that tend to arise, help resolve different team perspectives and perhaps challenge your thinking in a way that you will find beneficial.

THE FINISHED MAP

A finished map looks like an organizational chart, yet instead of having boxes with names, it has boxes with challenges in it. It also has a top box that does not contain a challenge.

This top box is about the benefits which will accrue to the team if it achieves the challenges. In motivational terms, it is useful to keep in front of teams the benefits of their future achievement. These benefits, however, should be suggested by the team, otherwise they could have little value!

In motivational terms, it is useful to keep in front of teams the benefits of their future achievement.

A finished map would look like the example in Figure 8.7.

You may remember that we start each challenge with 'How can we'. The 'we' needs to be defined for each challenge as there may be a different set of people involved. If a challenge passes out of control of any member of the team, it should not be on the map.

Kaizen teams can easily adopt the challenge approach. The 'we' equals members of the Kaizen team. The Kaizen team can, by following the mapping technique, reach an agreed consensus on its own issues and connect its own challenges to higher organization challenges. As a side benefit, it will produce a map it can use as a communication aid about what the team does.

Figure 8.7

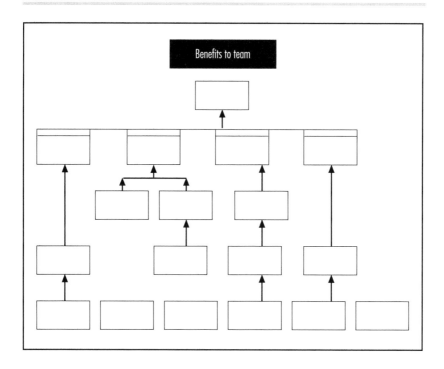

DIRECTING/RE-DIRECTING
A KAIZEN TEAM

Let us now go back to how to re-direct a Kaizen team. If either the team or the organizational direction is unclear, or both are unclear, then there is value in mapping out challenges and connecting them. Making the connections may be enough to re-direct (and rejuvenate) a team.

If a structure is already in place that strongly connects the team's direction to the overall direction, the only problems that occur will be when the overall direction changes.

In mapping terms, 'change' represents a higher challenge being changed which will change the challenges underneath it. This can have consequences for the Kaizen teams below. By having a map though, you can explain where the change has occurred and why it has occurred. You can then involve the appropriate teams in redesigning their part of the map. There is nothing like participation to assist in gaining commitment to a new reality!

There is nothing like participation to assist in gaining commitment to a new reality!

Sounds good, but does it work?

My experience suggests the process can totally engage teams at every level.

At the organizational level, the mapping technique has variously been described as 'the missing link in business planning', 'a brilliant strategic and communication aid', 'a technique to take companies through to the new millennium'. As a facilitator, it has been interesting to watch the amount of sharing going on as teams debate and agree their issues.

At a team level, it can clarify the thinking of the team, promote information sharing and unite behind a path of action. It can also uncover blocks to action and items outside the team's control. However, the method's power is to give the team the opportunity to take action by rewriting challenges into the 'How can we influence . . .' style. Once a team is clear on its map, it can then move into problem solving and if this is done in a participative way, great enjoyment can result.

It has also been interesting to note just how unclear the average team can be on what it is aiming to do. There is often an intuitive sense of how certain activities connect, yet until the connections are shared in an open logical approach then it is difficult to motivate people towards them. The mapping process straightens out intuition into a pathway.

The approach can also be used for innovation. The Centre for Research in Applied Creativity in Canada, which is run by Professor Min Basadur, has a particular mapping approach to innovation which has been used successfully with countless teams, particularly in the food process industry. If you have sophisticated processes where even small improvements can make substantial savings, then his Simplex[2] method is excellent. The author is an associate of the Europe Japan Centre and can provide further information.

Starting to use the mapping technique

If team direction or redirection is an issue for you now, then, in theory, you have a choice of two starting points: the Board level or the team level. In practice, the real challenge may be 'How can I influence senior management to review this technique?' or 'How can I revitalize the team?'. The reality may be more about getting others to take notice of the technique.

Fortunately, there is one thing you can do which is relatively easy. Whether the issue is in your team or another, have an 'away day' on the technique with your team. Not only will you be better able to assess the technique, you will find it easier to influence others once you have done it yourself. Even on the away day you can use the technique to check whether your team is dealing with the priority questions and examine how the technique fits in with other techniques that are motivational.

SUMMARY

In redirecting a team:

- review the nature of the problem
- establish whether the problem is organizational or team-based or both
- understand the enabling laws in organizations
- learn how to put objectives, purposes and activities into Challenge form
- test challenges for resilience
- connect challenges together to form a map
- use the map to give you a new direction or connect to other maps
- re-do the map if change affects any part of it.

Notes

1.   Ries, A. and Trout, J. *The 22 Immutable Laws of Marketing*, HarperCollins

2.   Basadur, M. *The Power of Innovation*, FT Pitman

CHAPTER 9

Stress and Turbulence –
Steadying the Kaizen Team

ANNIE ZLOTNICK

Associate, Europe Japan Centre

ALL ORGANIZATIONS OPERATE IN ENVIRONMENTS which create stress. This chapter helps readers understand the nature and manifestation of stress at work. Team membership is inherently stressing, and the chapter helps explain how negative stress can be avoided or dealt with and how positive stress can be encouraged.

INTRODUCTION

Every day 270,000 British workers are off work due to stress-related illnesses, costing employers around £8 billion a year. Researchers at the University of Manchester reported in 1997 that more than 60 per cent of occupations now have higher stress levels than they had 12 years ago. This is mainly attributed to redundancies, job insecurity, longer working hours and heavier workloads.

Stress has been the buzzword leading up to the millennium. We cannot live with it nor can we live without it. What is it anyway? Stress is a human condition, not a pathological one. It can be defined as anything which interferes with a person's physical or mental wellbeing. The interference can be a threat to the body and mind. Animals that we are, we respond to a threat with a fight or flight pattern. We want to fight or run away. Modern humans that we are, we cannot often use either of these avenues and the resulting stress is the body's way of handling the ambivalent response that our society demands. After all, it would not be a good idea to start a fistfight every time you are threatened and running away is often not a satisfactory or useful response. So we internalize our response and the anxiety we experience manifests itself in physical and psychological ways.

When the human body is placed under stress, the production of certain hormones increases. This results in noticeable changes in heart rate, blood pressure and activity. The body is programmed to handle this in short doses but it can be extremely damaging in the long run. Ailments resulting from long-term stress can be physical or psychological. Everyday symptoms such as irritability and mood swings may be noticeable and attributed to a bad day. However, the resulting illnesses can account for 60 per cent of absenteeism in the UK workplace.

POSITIVE AND NEGATIVE STRESS

The causes of stress are often referred to as stressors. Stressors can be environmental, for example, the pollution and noise of increased urbanization. Stressors can be personal: poor relationships, difficulties in families; and stressors can be work-related – actually caused by the type of work or the type of working environment. Changing roles in society have also created problems with conflicting obligations to family, work and self all competing for attention. For women in particular while the role of carer has not completely vanished, the role of breadwinner has taken more of a centre stage. This phenomenon also has an effect on men whose expectations of female partners, friends and colleagues have to change almost too quickly to understand.

These stressors can be classed as negative stressors when we feel that we can have little or no control over the situation. It appears that our perception of having control in a difficult situation can result in less negative stress or even in positive stress. It is the influence of these real or perceived threats that can produce a low-grade slowly erosive type of stress. Problems seem to arise when people feel that they are not able to cope. Workplace stress has been summed up by Susan Cartwright and Cary Cooper in their book *Managing Workplace Stress* (Sage 1997) as being primarily caused by the fundamentals of change, lack of control and high workload. They warn that workplace stress will increase in the next millennium due to rapid change in organizations and the lack of job security with the loss of the job-for-life.

Workplace stress will increase in the next millennium due to rapid change in organizations and the lack of job security with the loss of the job-for-life.

Yet we need stress to live. We need stress to motivate and to create. How many of us say that we work well under pressure? Referred to as positive stress it gives us a buzz and generates energy. It may be stressful but it may be exhilarating, like bungee jumping. We can work well under pressure but a lot will depend on who we are. The popular theories that guided a lot of our thinking divide individuals into type A and type B personalities; those who thrive on stress as opposed to individuals who tend to be relaxed. We used to tell the type A active individuals to try to relax and our overly relaxed type B friends to speed up. The advice is no longer given as we recognize individual differences and the fact that telling someone to relax will often increase the stress levels. People may be drawn to particular types of jobs which by definition may be stressful, e.g. fire fighters, surgeons, police, traders on the stock market floor who flourish under the cut and thrust of their jobs.

The strategy of the future seems to focus around recognizing stress that is negative or harmful and stress which is positive and motivating.

The strategy of the future seems to focus around recognizing stress that is negative or harmful and stress which is positive and motivating. One way to do this is to recognize the symptoms of harmful stress. These include: headaches, back aches, difficulty breathing, high blood pressure, insomnia, digestive disorders, ulcers and colitis.

Psychological signs include becoming overly emotional or aggressive in difficult situations, loss of interest in personal activities or appearance, difficulty concentrating or making decisions and a feeling of low self-esteem.

Negative stress can kill and it is interesting to note that the Japanese have officially recognized a condition called *Karoshi* – death from stress caused by too much work. Still, we humans can cope with a great deal of stress.

Signs of positive stress are increased excitement, extra energy, ability to think clearly or creatively and a need to continue at a fast pace in order to achieve something. This may be experienced by scientists on the verge of an historical break-through or a team on the verge of a successful project.

THE EFFECT OF STRESS ON TEAMS

Part of the challenge for teams is that teams are made up of people and people can be stressed and this stress can affect their teammates. The disruptive team member may not be the loud and aggressive individual, but rather the quieter passive but hostile, angry person whose domestic problems are getting the better of him or her. So how do teams cope with the stress of individuals?

Case Study

A team member committed suicide during a long holiday break. Other team members who initially sought solace from one another were offered counselling. Unfortunately the counsellor was not well trained and his perceived intrusion into the life of the team members resulted in another team member having a nervous breakdown.

This is a sad illustration of the domino effect of harmful individual stress. The first step seems to be recognition of stress as a factor of life and recognizing it as both a positive and negative force for continuous improvement. This was the tactic taken by Zeneca Pharmaceuticals who promoted the awareness of stress throughout their organization and offered support where required, as well as training staff in stress management skills. Critical to this initiative was the fact that stress was now on the agenda and one could speak openly about it. Very often it is considered a sign of weakness to talk about stress. No one wants anyone to think that they are not up to the job.

Very often it is considered a sign of weakness to talk about stress. No one wants anyone to think that they are not up to the job.

Concerns which are not of a personal nature and cause stress amongst employees include lack of control over workload, lack of trust or appreciation at work; lack of feedback about performance. Being able to speak about these issues defuses the situation before it gets out of control. This should be an ideal strategy for teams – to allow the openness that will result in recognizing stress for what it is and allowing members to support one another or respond appropriately. Belonging to a team should offer its members the opportunity to tell their fellow team members of their stresses at home.

While one may not approve of bringing problems to work, the opposite is also true. Burying problems and not recognizing them for what they are leaves its mark on the whole team. Teams need to acknowledge their human side and though one would not recommend dwelling on individual problems, sending someone for the necessary support would help the team move on.

TEAM-GENERATED STRESS

Now a look at the stress that teams themselves can generate. In turbulent environments with rapid technological change and high levels of competition, greater flexibility is required of organizations and their teams. Teams must evolve their own creative solutions to both threats (negative stress) and opportunities (positive stress).

Teams by their very nature are difficult places to be, not only for the first time team members but also for members from different disciplines participating in cross-functional teams. The first moment of stress occurs in the very formation of the team. New teams are like newborn children requiring a time before they are weaned away from their former work habits and systems. Leadership and support from the parent organization is crucial at this point and the team needs to feel secure in order to do its work without repercussions.

On a macro level, expectations are often not spelled out and communication channels with the parent organization are often unclear and tenuous. Are teams set up due to the latest fad? How will they interact with the rest of the organization? Can the organization uphold the team culture? Questions that remain unanswered as the team is selected and is in the process of forming are as follows.

- How long will the team exist?
- What will be the team focus?
- How will decisions be made and how will these decision impact on the rest of the organization?
- To whom do team members owe their loyalty? What will the training strategy be? (for ongoing team maintenance).

Answering these questions early on can ensure a smoother path for team growth.

Case Study

One particular company emphasizes in its hiring practices the flat structure of its organization and the lack of promotion possibilities. It is a team situation for individuals wishing to work in a creative, continuously improving environment. The strategy, which does not dissuade many applicants, also allows for a less stressful team situation, as those recruited recognize that the motivation will come from within the team.

Team leaders are often unsure of their role and though they wish the team to thrive are still responsible for the bottom line and customer expectations. The team leader, a crucial person at this time, often disappears for the following reasons.

- Confusion – how much direction does the team need? How much should I be involved? Is it not better to let them get on with it?

- The fear of being accused of being the old-style autocratic manager who cannot sit back and truly empower the team so that the *laissez-faire* approach seems to be the best.
- The fear of not having the requisite skills to guide the team and requiring additional training and support. This is the stress experienced in the forming stages as the team tries to cope with change.

Case Study

A team of three years' standing admitted a new member with great reluctance. The new member was not keen to be in a team environment and preferred to keep to herself. The situation was exacerbated as the new team member was also the only black team member and the entire situation took on ugly racial overtones. The team leader did not know whether to intervene or how much to intervene. Sadly her inaction took its toll and by the time the team demanded a facilitator for the breakdown in team communication both the new member and the team leader had to leave and the team had to reform.

While one may think that the performing stage should be plain sailing, this may not be the case. Teams are very often being created and recreated, this process of *Kaizen* (continuous improvement) requires continuous evaluation and re-evaluation, which will result in change, however small. Change will create its own stress. Even positive change brings its own stress. Belonging to a team will then almost by definition become a stressful experience. The stressors will often stay the same; it is our reaction and coping that can change. The changes offered by *Kaizen* need to elicit positive stressors that can galvanize the team and move it on. These can be changes that come from the team as opposed to those imposed on the team. These are changes for which the team has developed ongoing coping mechanisms.

Case Study

A hospital trust management team was plagued by the white papers coming from the government and forever had to rally their staff around the impending crisis, leaving the day-to-day operations to sink. Their solution had to be a task force to monitor imminent governmental moves so that the necessary people could be mobilized to deal with new directives as soon as they came on board.

This is in direct contrast to changes that are out of the control of the team, which can often destroy the team.

Case Study

A local authority was determined to reduce bureaucracy and create smaller groups based in areas to better serve the local populace. The resulting team-building days exposed the bad feeling still remaining from a strike, which had divided the staff years before. The team-building exercise itself was painful as staff confronted each other and tried to find creative solutions to enable them to work together in a better atmosphere. The result was a true feeling of having achieved something – a way forward and a way to work together. This was derailed when the local government decided that three geographical designations were not as they wished and the team was disbanded to be reformed elsewhere and with new colleagues. While team members learned from their experience, the stress of being reformed resulted in depression and a hankering for what may have been.

Similar problems exist when companies merge and fail to take on board the two differing cultures of the organizations. As with many mergers of this type one company will became the dominant company and all staff will have to deal with a culture of blame and bureaucracy. This group of people will have a steep learning curve with some individuals having to leave because they will not be able to cope with the stress.

Case Study

Two teams had been working in tandem in two organizations during the merger process. This was seen as a way forward for their eventual collaboration. Both teams had agreed upon the team leader and this was to be a successful merger and an example for the rest of the company. Lo and behold, working in tandem did not account for the two differing team cultures with regard to such basic issues as time keeping and record keeping. The team leader was seen as promoting her team and their ways. Instead of being a single team the battle lines were being drawn.

As teams develop and continually improve, the following stresses begin to emerge:

- disruptive team members for whom the changes are too fast or too soon or disruptive behaviour which wasn't confronted in the initial formation stages
- disabling team habits that develop – members showing up late for meetings or missing them all together
- the difficulty in decision making because a full consensus is necessary to make every decision and the team is often bogged down in the decision-making process
- difficulty in refocusing due to new information or changes in other teams or parts of the company
- boundary issues – what is yours, mine and ours? The ownership of varied team member contributions and offerings.

TURNING NEGATIVE STRESS INTO POSITIVE STRESS

Now that we have identified the major underlying causes of team stress we have to turn to solutions.

Create communication channels

The first and most important solution is creating an environment that allows communication about stress. Teams must, in their formative stages, discuss stresses, fears and anxieties with a trained leader or outside consultant. This was the point mentioned earlier in regard to individual stress. While not every individual will feel comfortable dealing with his or her personal stress in the context of the entire team, channels for handling stress must be created.

The team leader should be approachable on any issue. Agreement between the team leader and the individual employee on methods of handling stress must include references to the team. These references must include information sharing (to the extent made possible by confidentiality) as well as ways of minimizing the impact of stress on the team. These two points are crucial in preventing the rumour mill and resentment from overtaking the team. What could be worse than whispered discussions on why X is not carrying his or her weight? This also begins to assure a blameless culture where there is no finger pointing at team meetings.

Case Study

A team was having difficulty in confronting a disruptive member. While the views of this member were valued, her acerbic delivery, as well as her disregard of fellow team members' views, were contributing to rancour within the team. The team leader offered members two ways of dealing with the situation. They could either work it out as a team or the team leader would take it up with Personnel on an individual basis. The team requested that they handle this as a team with an outside facilitator. The team leader has agreed to this even though she feels that it may still end up with Personnel. She sees this as team learning as well as the team's opportunity to reassert itself and its rules.

Recognize that change causes stress

A next and linked step would be to acknowledge and identify the negative and positive stress that would inevitably be created by *Kaizen's* emphasis on continuous improvement. Familiarity with the reaction to change described by Darryl R. Conner in his book *Managing at the Speed of Change* (Villard Books, NY 1993) is a place to start. His model of reaction to change describes denial, anger, bargaining, depression and acceptance based on the work of Dr Elisabeth Kubler-Ross on death and dying.

Indeed, change can be a form of bereavement and will contain elements of denial, anger, bargaining and depression before acceptance takes root.

Indeed, change can be a form of bereavement and will contain elements of denial, anger, bargaining and depression before acceptance takes root. However, the reaction to change can also follow a positive curve of uninformed optimism, informed pessimism, hopeful realism and informed optimism. The learning curve of *Kaizen* can follow this positive change curve with the use of key communications, involvement of the workforce, setting an example and encouraging and participating with staff in their feelings as described above. It is then that one can expect a commitment to change. An awareness of the ups and downs of the change process would point to a feeling of normalcy when experiencing the same uncertainties.

Case Study

On many training sessions I have found that the mere presentation of the effects of change leads participants to immediately identify where they have been and where they are going. They are also clearly delighted to find colleagues in different fields and areas going through the same thing.

Give some breathers

Next on the agenda for the team would be breathers, or respite between change initiatives. The team does need to take a deep breath and celebrate its successes before embarking on any other improvements and the change impact associated with those improvements. If team members call for time out after a particularly arduous period – they deserve it. Sitting back and celebrating successes is an energizing process, which paves the way for further improvement and recognition of positive stress – the motivating type that gives THE BUZZ. Teams need built-in breathers – not only the types that come with waves of change. Whether these breaks are once or twice a year, or more often, they give the team time to reassess, to leave the immediate and concentrate on the future. Regular 'how are we doing' checks will reveal any problems – real or perceived – by the team. Reassessing priorities allows for greater team effectiveness.

At times additional training or communication with senior man-agement is necessary to bolster the team. The team may be asked to do different tasks on these away days to stretch their abilities. At some point the team leader may need to decide how best to proceed – either allow and further empower the team to seek solutions or offer solutions where the team may be less able, i.e. interface with other teams or oper-ations not within easy reach.

Any problem-solving exercise is crucial to the *Kaizen* culture, as it identifies not only the problems that need immediate solutions but often identifies future problems. The point is not to be side-tracked by future problems but to solve the problems at hand with a note to work on future problems in light of present solutions. It is important to indi-cate when future problems may be solved so that the team can see their way clear to the future.

Keep motivating

Another way of avoiding the stress of uncertainty that may be experi-enced as a particular project winds down is to ensure that the team is constantly motivated. This is particularly important in an organization with a flat structure where advancement is not a real possibility.

Conferences, visits to other businesses in the same field as well as sharing in company information, motivates the team. These opportun-ities for creative thinking decrease negative stress and channel it into the positive stress of new ideas and challenges.

The role of the team leader

The role of the team leader in avoiding and dealing with stress is also crucial. A key role is the development of effective links between the team and the parent organization. The team's role must be a stable one within the organization.

Decisions on the interface between the team and the parent organization are most often left to the team leader as part of his or her role The team leader must also identify his or her role *vis-à-vis* the team's decision making. An autocratic decision by the leader will speed up a particular decision but destroy the team's ability for moving itself forward. Democratic decisions can encourage participation but will take longer. Consensus decisions will gain the team's unanimous support but will often be based in compromise to assure full participation. Democratic decisions allow the teams to move forward with their tasks while consensus decisions allow the team to grow. Guidance as to the type of decision making must be clearly demarcated.

SUMMARY

The work of the team must include ensuring team maintenance. Teams will inevitably experience stress and this stress can either destroy or energize the team. Whether stress destroys or energizes the team will depend on the team's ability to

- deal with stress
- transform negative stress to positive stress
- be led by a leader well equipped to deal with the vicissitudes of team life.

PART FOUR

Kaizen Teams in the Future

CHAPTER 10

The Changing Strategic Environment

Introduction

Drivers of the Competitive Environment

How Organizations are Responding

Summary

MICHAEL COLENSO

Associate, Europe Japan Centre

THIS CHAPTER EXPLORES THE MAJOR drivers of the contemporary organizational climate and especially the intensifying competitive environment. It outlines some of the generic strategic strengths which organizations are building to cope with this climate and it speculates on the value of *Kaizen*-driven teams to support these core capabilities.

INTRODUCTION

The way organizations deploy, task and use teams is changing quite substantially. These changes mirror not only the differing strategies organizations are pursuing, but a different environment in which they now operate. The classic model of a system in which value is added by employees and processes at various stages along a route which eventually leads to a satisfied customer, while still valid, represents too introspective a view of the organization. Such a view was tenable when the external environment was relatively predictable. Now an organization needs to see itself as a component of an extended value system which starts with suppliers, embraces the value adding activities of the organization, moves downstream to the customer and does so in an unstable and largely unpredictable competitive climate.

Dealing with this complexity, unpredictability or, as Drucker so presciently described it, discontinuity, means that organizations have to think about themselves quite differently in order to develop strategies for survival. This in turn affects the way they structure themselves, the use to which teams are put and the way they operate.

The phrase '*Kaizen* is not enough' mentioned by Chris Patrick in Chapter 2 has been attributed to various vice presidents of Toyota. It arises, I suspect, because Toyota needs a rallying cry to alert its employees to the fact that the game has changed in the competitive economic climate. By using the cry, and apparently using it a lot, Toyota seeks to galvanize its workers not only to renewed effort, but to effort of a qualitatively different kind.

What we know of Toyota's current strategic intent is that the company looks upon itself as a global player aspiring to a share of the world's car market exceeding 10 per cent. It will achieve this by creating a series of regional manufacturing hubs, each of which will make cars which are customized to the hub's local markets. While doing this it also aims to cut its build costs and radically reduce its order-to-delivery time. The company is in the process of a $13 billion investment to achieve this.

Toyota's vision is both thrilling and daunting, and achieving it probably implies a radical redesign of the company. It will affect how the company organizes itself, how it thinks about itself; its priorities will change, its behaviour must change. On the face of it, what Toyota is saying is that approaching this from the context of incremental improvement, which lies at the heart of *Kaizen*, is at least inappropriate, at worst a deadly distraction from the job at hand. It seems probable to me that the real truth of the '*Kaizen* is not enough' statement implies not a rejection of *Kaizen* but the need to bring the additional ingredient of transformation to the corporate culture.

Two views have prevailed about the origin of the universe. One, the Big Bang theory, the other, the Steady State theory. One of these theories is correct, probably Big Bang. Toyota appears to be signalling that, like the universe, its future appearance will be more of a Big Bang phenomenon than a Steady State evolution.

Nor is Toyota's view unique, it is not even unusual among large global corporations or among the gurus of organizational thinking. The 'in' words are 'reinvention' and 'transformation', and the 'in' thinking is that organizations do not grow by extrapolating from past successes but rather from seizing the opportunities presented by the marketplace and building position in them as rapidly as possible. These marketplaces need not even be the primary or usual areas of the organization's business. We have seen Virgin, for example, move from the record business to airline operator, through wedding dress supplier to financial services provider, to name but a few of its transformations. We have seen Carlton Communications move from mail order house through video duplication, to television producer, to broadcaster and now, linked with its long-term rival Granada, in pursuit of the digital television opportunity.

In both cases the core business of the organization has changed over a relatively short period of time. Both organizations now derive their major revenues and/or profits from businesses quite different from those which provided them ten years ago. This is 'reinvention' in action. In Virgin's case, the businesses it has entered have often been radically different and seemingly unrelated. It has been able to do this because of the powerful association of value, quality, modernity and style which are vested in its brand name. Carlton, on the other hand, has acquired or built businesses in closely adjacent markets, presenting a much more coherent picture of acquisition and expansion.

Thinking and acting, revolution-not-evolution, reinvention-not-incremental-expansion, besides serving as a handy credo for corporate vice presidents and for management gurus, does reflect a sea change in the competitive economic climate. What is driving this change, and what are the dynamics which have changed the game?

DRIVERS OF THE
COMPETITIVE ENVIRONMENT

Identifying the drivers or causal factors of these changes helps understand their significance to the organization. It enables one to think more clearly about how an organization can position itself as part of an extended value system operating in an unpredictable climate. Each of the drivers interacts with the others and your list may not correspond to mine, though we will probably both recognize the effects. My list is:

- a more demanding customer
- technology
- globalization
- proliferation of stakeholders.

Let us look at each of these in turn.

The customer

It is arguably one of the legacies of Kaizen with its focus on customers and the continuous improvement of quality, that we now have a much more demanding customer with a higher expectation of quality, convenience, range, choice and added value.

Most organizations now deal with customers who have the luxury of extremely wide choice. The rules of mass production have changed since the day that Henry Ford offered Model Ts in any colour people wanted so long as it was black. Technology has made possible the low cost manufacture of quite short runs of goods. It has enabled a high degree of customization, versioning and special build. In services sectors too, technology's ability to access information rapidly and to reproduce it inexpensively enables the provision of more varied and specialist services.

Confronted with burgeoning choice, customers have been quick to exercise it and even to pay a little more for the luxury of it. This has led into the 'twigging' of markets with a number of smaller and more specialist shoots coming off the main product/service branch. Twigging in turn spawns more specialist players in the markets and a further proliferation of market opportunities. Customer choice enables niches to survive or not depending on the scale of operations, the efficiency of the provider, and the degree of value the customer perceives to have been added in relation to price.

It is arguably one of the legacies of *Kaizen* with its focus on customers and the continuous improvement of quality, that we now have a much more demanding customer with a higher expectation of quality, convenience, range, choice and added value. Keeping that customer happy and loyal in turn means that organizations have consistently to increase added value, improve quality and to innovate.

Some of the consequences of this are that organizations must know their customers extremely well. They must be capable of an accelerated product/service development cycle, and they must expect a shorter product life cycle. Competitive advantage, when gained, lasts for a very short period of time, and markets are rarely dominated by a single supplier for long.

Technology

Some of the effect of technology in manufacturing and information retrieval has been outlined above but the impact is far larger, affecting not only the goods and services we provide, but how we bring them to market, and the internal processes we use to run our organizations. On the other side of the equation, the customer is also using technology to shop, compare prices, access comparative performance data and so on. Further the customer is increasingly able to shop internationally, bypassing the provider's distribution channels and making nonsense of regional pricing differentials.

Internet marketing is developing fast and the growth of e-commerce means that for the cost of a website, any organization can enter a market and make a global offering. The barriers to entering many markets are falling and risk is being minimized by the falling entry cost. Of course, not all products and services lend themselves to e-commerce, nor can all markets be accessed, but *Fortune* magazine devotes a substantial part of its December 1998 issue to organizations which are not merely marketing and selling through the Internet, but actually modelling themselves around the special requirements of e-commerce.

Right now almost all e-commerce passes through a personal computer which still requires a capital investment and some operator expertise. When it is linked into the television/edutainment complex through a user-friendly remote control, we will see yet another unprecedented selling and marketing opportunity. This opportunity will arise before we have properly learned to exploit the existing one.

As organizations link their internal IT systems through upstream supplier networks, and downstream channels and distributor networks, right through to their customers, we can again anticipate new business models and new organizational structures emerging.

It is not the purpose of this chapter to enter the realms of predictive futurology but the concept of changing organizational models helps us understand how radical are the changes being driven by technology. The retailing model, for example, has moved from the high street to the shopping centre to the superstore. It is reasonable to expect that the retailing business model of the future will also be radically altered by e-commerce. The employment model of a workforce reporting to a location for a fixed working day is now superseded by a model based on outsourcing, hot desking, computer-cottage approaches; this is again enabled by technology.

In short, the fusion of telecommunications and computing has altered the world. Those changes have not ceased and the impending fusion of this with the existing television industry will change it again. Small wonder that the pundits use words like 'reinvention'.

Globalization

This is a convenient word which means two things. First it means that there are substantial **opportunities** for any organization to become a global player (via Internet being a fast, cheap way). Second it means that the competitive climate has become entirely **unpredictable.** You are never certain who your competition is or even where it is located.

Globalization implies that any supplier can trade anywhere round the world. The Internet, credit card facilities, and international delivery systems (some electronic) all make global trading a feasible option in a number of industries. Then too, as the tariff barriers of the past increasingly fall, goods and money also pass more freely through the global networks. Finally, the search of large amounts of international capital for new markets, new opportunities and new businesses encourages the development of global markets. As the euro becomes a tradable, comparable, fixed value currency for some 300 million first world consumers too, the effects of globalization are likely to be even more widely felt.

All these developments make it harder to monitor the climate in which an organization operates. It makes the competitive climate less predictable; it means that the organization has to be faster on its feet to recognize and enact change. Arguably it is this organizational responsiveness which may make the difference between success and failure.

Stakeholders

Beside looking at the organization as part of an extended value system, we have also to consider how it fits with the beliefs of its major stakeholders. Almost all studies of the organization of the future identify an increasing number of powerful groups of stakeholders who influence how the organization must behave. Stakeholders range from its owners, through to its customers and on the way touch the press and the media, the industry's reputation, the various lobbies with which it may be involved, the professional bodies to which it and its employees belong, sometimes government, its local and global 'citizenship' responsibilities, standards, health and safety and the law.

The evidence of studies of organizations who have gained the Malcolm Baldrige award, one of the USA's most prestigious quality awards, is that those which handle all these multiple stakeholders effectively are those most likely to succeed. Designing an organization which is in touch with its stakeholders, able to anticipate their reactions to what it does, responsive to changing beliefs and values is no mean task.

Responding to the aspirations and needs of its employees alone is a major challenge, but a necessary one as increasingly, employees become the means of differentiation and strategy implementation. Line managers need to become strategists themselves as well as coaches and mentors. This implies development, training, learning, empowerment, as well as executive competence.

The quality of the organization's intellectual capital, its internal knowledge, competence and capability lies at the heart of its ability to survive. Developing this intellectual capital must stand at the centre of all strategies.

The quality of the organization's intellectual capital, its internal knowledge, competence and capability lies at the heart of its ability to survive.

HOW ORGANIZATIONS ARE RESPONDING

Possibly the most important attribute an organization needs for long-term survival is responsiveness: the ability to spot a trend and move fast to exploit it if the trend presents an opportunity, or to compensate if the trend is threatening. This looks like an athletic organization, one that is fast on its feet, one that is alert to the game, one that has stamina and the will to win.

Translating this vision into reality appears to revolve around three main areas of focus:

- **structure** – the component parts of the organization and how it is wired together
- **control methods** – broadly, how the organization is directed to implement its strategy
- **culture** – the beliefs or values systems which facilitate the implementation of strategy.

Let us look at each of these in turn.

Structure

Possibly the most important attribute an organization needs for long-term survival is responsiveness: the ability to spot a trend and move fast to exploit it if the trend presents an opportunity, or to compensate if the trend is threatening.

First of all the athletic organization is much flatter with fewer layers of hierarchy. Many organizations have gone this route to some advantage. The more layers the message has to pass through, the less accurate it becomes at each repetition, according to Drucker, producing twice the noise and conveying half the content.

Another major characteristic of the athletic organization is that there is ample facility provided for cross-functional activity. There is no general rule as to whether the organization should be organized on a functional basis, on a customer-focus basis, on a process focus, on a market focus or on a matrix basis. All of these bases of organization seem to work depending on the nature of what the organization does. What is important though, is that whatever the basis, operating departments must not be allowed to develop into a series of independent silos (airtight grain-houses) and cross-functionality must be enabled. This is, of course, one of the great strengths which *Kaizen* teams can bring to the structure.

Teams are one of the means of compensating for the disadvantages which are characteristic of any of the structural options. Quite often we get vertical operating departments as the units of organization, and cross-functional teams as the catalysts for change and improvement. When such teams achieve synergy, this provides a powerful cardiovascular system for our organization-as-athlete.

Increasingly, too, we see that while organizations themselves are getting larger and larger through merger and acquisition, at the same time the operating components are getting smaller. This facilitates team building and hence productivity.

We are also seeing organizations becoming very clear about where their core strengths or core competencies lie. The concept of the broadly based multifunctional integrated organization is waning and instead time is being spent on identifying those skills which are essential to the organization to enable it to fulfil its purpose on the one hand and to implement its strategy on the other. Functions or activities not essential to these two requirements are being spun off or outsourced. This leaves a highly focused central core which potentially operates more effectively.

Control methods

By 'control' I mean the systems the organization uses to implement its strategy. The relationship between what employees actually do and the organization's strategy is usually established by a unit manager, team leader or supervisor. The means by which this is most commonly achieved is by agreeing objectives and monitoring performance against them. Objectives are used to focus the employee on what needs to be done, and systems, procedures, company rules, etc. regulate how it will be done.

Tried and proven as this system is, there is evidence that things move so fast now that the objectives of six months ago look strangely inappropriate when they come to be reviewed. It seems to me that management by objectives works well in stable and slowly evolving environments. It may well be too ponderous a system in the faster moving climate in which most organizations now operate.

The currently accepted wisdom is for devolved decision making and greater employee empowerment. Frequently this devolution and empowerment is not individualized but vested in a team with collective responsibility for what they do. Unquestionably many organizations derive great benefit from operating in this way. It can be a recipe for anarchy, however, and quite unfair on employees, if no context is provided for the decision making and no parameters established for empowerment.

In Chapter 8 on re-directing *Kaizen* teams, John Hall provides tools for aligning the activity of teams more closely with the strategic intent of the organization. It seems to me though that we must look upon alignment as a primary means of controlling the organization because it provides the team and /or the individual employee with the context of decision making.

Alignment is best achieved by involvement. In other words, the organization's strategy and planning becomes a collective activity rather than a plan emerging fully formed from the executive offices. The Japanese system of *hoshin kanri* provides an effective process for achieving this and also moves some way to building the bridge between continuous incremental improvement on the one hand, and the need for breakthrough and reinvention on the other.

The system works when the organization has taken time and participative effort to create a vision of where it will be in the future. The importance of this precondition becomes clear when you understand that the words *hoshin kanri* are used to mean 'compass/navigation'; without a destination (the vision) we cannot use our compass productively and we cannot navigate at all.

With the vision in position and shared by all employees, the basic planks of the strategic intent can be laid. These broadly define the markets in which the organization intends to play, the nature of the products and services it will offer and the means by which the organization will differentiate itself from others. The strategic intent is then passed through the organization so that the operating units can convert it into an operating plan. In the process the strategic intent is tested, honed, developed and refined. Graphically the process looks like this:

Figure 10.1 *Hoshin kanri at work*

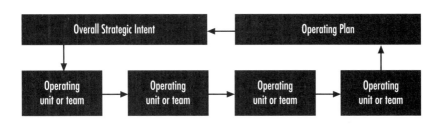

What delivers the control is that as people work with the broad brush strategic intent they come to understand the realities of implementation and to test those realities against the detailed knowledge each has of his or her functions and his or her particular job. It is from this planning and testing that alignment is developed, a context for decision making is established and the relationships between what I do day-to-day and the overall strategy become obvious.

Control emerges because members of the organization are pulled towards the vision. Individuals and teams make decisions in the longer term strategic context rather than simply fixing day-to-day problems. Opportunities are spotted to contribute to the strategic intent, priorities are fixed by criteria which support the strategy and so on. In short we have a responsive, athletic organization.

Usually what emerges in the *hoshin kanri* process is that there are two categories of things the organization must achieve: things at which we must get better; and breakthroughs we must achieve. Some organizations call the first category the *Kaizen*s and the second category the Hoshins.

Here at last we see the synthesis of the breakthrough, reinvention school of thought and the incremental improvement school of thought. The reality is that the responsive organization must be capable of both, an athletic 'biathlon'. I suspect that Toyota knows this.

Culture

In an earlier chapter I have defined organizational culture as the belief systems the employees of an organization share about what gets rewarded around here, what gets punished, and what gets ignored. We looked also at the congruence between a *Kaizen* culture and the sort of culture we need to run a modern organization.

Most organizations find that coupling teaming with participative strategy development and planning affects the culture very positively. Many also find that the principles of *Kaizen* provide a ready-made code of conduct which helps in interpersonal and inter-organizational processes. But one of the really important additions to the contemporary organization is to cultivate a need for learning, and for individual development.

Most organizations find that coupling teaming with participative strategy development and planning affects the culture very positively.

Teams constitute an especially excellent forum for learning. Serving as a member of a team is, itself, developmental, and as the team confronts and solves problems, all members learn and develop in the process. Successful teams spend time on retrospection asking: 'What did we do that made it work? What did we do that made it fail? How might we have done it better?'

Developing a learning culture in an organization requires creating the opportunities by secondment, appointing people to project teams, job rotation and so on. It requires matching of individual abilities to organizational needs and investing in bridging the gaps. Above all it requires a culture which rewards learning and continuously reinforces the need for it.

Intellectual capital still does not show on the balance sheet of an organization. But it usually does show in the competence the organization has to respond to its markets and adapt to its environment. The way it shows is usually in accelerated growth and greater productivity.

SUMMARY

The drivers which are changing the competitive environment are:

- *customers* – demanding better quality, larger choice and improved value
- *technology* – affecting products and services, internal processes, the way in which we bring our goods and services to markets
- *globalization* – intensifying competition and making our operating environment less predictable
- *multiple stakeholders* – having to be taken seriously and kept happy; this includes employees who must be developed as a primary asset.

So the strategic properties of the responsive, athletic organization are:

- it must be fast on its feet, capable of quick change
- it must have a transparent structure with cross functionality built into its operations
- it must have a supportive culture of devolved decision making and empowerment
- to build this culture there should be a high level of participation in strategy preparation and planning
- it must be able to sustain continuous incremental development – the *Kaizen*s
- simultaneously it must be focusing on opportunities for breakthrough, reinvention and transformation – the Hoshins
- above all it must be developing its intellectual capital by developing its people through opportunity, training and formal education – a learning organization.

Table 10.2 which follows is a matrix advising on the use of teams in trying to achieve this athletic, responsive organization. The aim in the end is to produce flexibility in the organization, good listening skills (to each other and to the marketplace), to make the organization more receptive to change and more open to newness.

It is arguable whether teams lie at the heart of reinvention; the evidence is that they probably do not. The impetus for the substantial change needed to alter an organization radically seems more frequently to arise from the top. It is quite clear though, that given the impetus, teams provide an executive instrument for enacting change provided they are used selectively and with precision. Effective use depends on the organization's ability to task them properly and to keep them aligned with the organization's strategic intent.

The environment in which teams must now operate is changing too and the next two chapters deal with the virtual team and the continuing effect of technology on team development.

Table 10.2 *Using teams to create a responsive organization*

Strategic purpose	Benefit sought	Tasking	Composition	Timing
Lower operating cost	Process reengineering	Examine (designated) processes to simplify, streamline and excise all non value-added elements	Cross-functional membership with 'hands on' experience of their own and adjacent processes	Fixed time scale 'x' months
Improve quality	Customer satisfaction Diminished warranty work	Raise quality to benchmarked levels	Cross-functional membership with 'hands on' experience of their own and adjacent processes	Ongoing with frequent reviews
New product	Additional profitable revenue stream at defined overhead and investment	Specify investment and expected revenue, also any constraints	Customer conscious imaginative members who know the capabilities of the organization	Fixed deadline not too far in the future
New markets	Additional revenue stream at defined profit and entry cost	Specify revenues sought, profit and allowable development cost	Analytical membership capable of detailed research and market analysis	Fixed deadline not too far in the future
Project management, e.g. product launch or special customer project	Successful on time completion Coordination of in-house and outsourced resources	Specific description of project with defined, quantified outcomes	Project stakeholders people who will be affected if they get it right or if they get it wrong	Determined by project deadline
Productivity	Greater throughput Usually involves converting an existing department to a team	Find the synergy, define the benefits sought (usually Quality or £)	Members of the department	Ongoing
Customer satisfaction	Improved customer retention	Ascertain components of customer satisfaction and design implementation	Usually cross functional, must be customer aware	Usually ongoing tracking of customer satisfaction as the goal posts move

CHAPTER 11

The Virtual Team

Introduction

What is Virtual or Remote Working?

Prerequisites for Introducing Remote Team Working

The Role of the Virtual Team Leader

Summary

ROBERT HERSOWITZ

Associate, Europe Japan Centre

AFTER DEFINING WHAT VIRTUAL TEAMS are and how they are different from other types of teams, Robert Hersowitz outlines the pitfalls and benefits of creating them. Detailed instructions follow for creating the virtual team with areas where particular care is needed highlighted. The chapter uses case examples and shares the experience, positive and negative, of others.

INTRODUCTION

The concept of virtual teams is very new to industry and commerce. Like most new phenomena in the era of change, the issues surrounding the setting up and running of these groups is in a state of transition and evolution. There are no fixed definitions about what a virtual team is. This is still linked to the classic definition of a team – which is 'a group of individuals who share a common goal'. In the case of virtual teams, the groups of individuals are not working face to face in the same venue. In fact in the current day and age of the new millennium, the configuration of group working is multifaceted.

There are now several different combinations of how people work together. They include:

- same place, same time
- different place, same time
- different place, different time.

Virtual teams can also be made up of:

- members who work for the same organization and who are spread around one country in different locations
- members who work for the same multinational organization spread across the globe
- members who represent different companies, suppliers and customers, some of whom may be in competition with each other but need to collaborate on different projects locally and internationally.

Most of this change in group working has been driven by the evolution of technology. Satellite communication, personal computers, modem links, the Internet and intranets have helped to bring about a world-wide economic revolution. Almost twenty years ago, commentators were beginning to write about this revolution. Alvin Tofler in his book *The Third Wave*, talked about the concept of the electronic cottage.

Today the electronic cottage is a reality and exists in every suburban street in most cities throughout the developed economies of the world. At the beginning of the 21st century we are at the most rudimentary stages of remote and virtual working. Our computers are powerful but not as powerful as they will still become. Nevertheless the impact of information technology on the future is irreversible and the challenge to every organization is how to deploy this incredible resource productively. One clear way forward is to learn how to work remotely.

WHAT IS VIRTUAL OR REMOTE WORKING?

When an organization makes the shift to remote working, it does so to promote efficiency and to cut costs. Information technology companies like Digital and Unisys lead the field. They have sold off millions of dollars' worth of property all over Europe and the USA. The cost of maintaining one manager in an office building costs approximately $12,000 per year. When the real estate has been sold off and the individual has been given a lap top computer, an ISDN telephone line at home and a budget to turn a bedroom into an office, it costs the company less than $5,000 per year to maintain this person. When this is executed and organized on a multiple scale, the concept of organized remote working pays huge dividends.

Remote working takes place when individuals and groups are networked together through technology. They may be located in the same building, across international borders, overseas or at home, in their vehicle or even on a plane or train or whilst they are sitting in a restaurant. The recurring theme which runs throughout the life and work of these people is 'networked remoteness'. This almost sounds like a contradiction in terms – yet when virtual teams are formed and conscientiously developed, they can become an extremely powerful and versatile asset to any organization.

Virtual teams – the benefits

Imagine an international organization where everything works like clockwork. Information and knowledge are transferred at the touch of a button. There is no need for delays in providing service and products. Deliveries are always on time as suppliers and customers are connected through the most efficient conduits of communication. Projects are seamlessly co-ordinated. Staff are empowered to make decisions and introduce relevant changes to processes and procedures. Customers are given accurate and timely information. Everything is well documented and information is easily accessible. Waste is reduced and sometimes completely eliminated. This is the vision of what could be and in some cases 'what is'. *Kaizen* and the Japanese concept of *muda* (identifying and eliminating waste) are important skill/competency assets for remotely structured organizations. The byword of such an organization is FLEXIBILITY. This is what well organized remote working and virtual teams can offer. There is no instant transformation to the state we have just described. The entire cultural transformation to virtual working is a painstaking process of change management and above all top management commitment, support and understanding. It is a way of working for the present and the future. Many 21st century organizations such as Otiken (Denmark) have embraced the concept of the spaghetti, fishnet or fluid matrix organization.

The entire cultural transformation to virtual working is a painstaking process of change management and above all top management commitment, support and understanding.

Characteristics of the fluid matrix

- non-hierarchical
- flat, networked teams and groups
- leaderless, or leadership from the centre of a network or hub when and where necessary
- managers are more involved with strategy, anticipating change and reshaping team activity to meet future needs
- informal group internal and external networking leads to a hot-house of creativity and innovation
- teams, not hierarchies do the real work
- group activity is *ad hoc* – forming, reforming and disappearing.

Unlike a rigid matrix, a fluid matrix is an organizational structure which allows a great deal of freedom and manoeuvrability. There are dotted line reporting responsibilities. The key factor, however, is constantly changing flexible teams, many of whom are working remotely or as virtual teams. These teams operate without old fashioned heroic leadership. They are self-managed teams where leadership rotates according to the current project or work requirement. Many of these teams embrace the culture of *Kaizen* or continuous improvement. Because these teams have matured into self-regulating bodies where everyone has access to information and the capability to acquire, practise and execute new skills, the increase in productivity and creativity can be very powerful.

The pitfalls of virtual working

Many organizations embrace the concept of virtual teams by accident. This could be because of the way they are organized. National distribution of goods and services requires the setting up of regional offices both inside one country but also in several countries. This is the natural evolution of virtual teams. In some cases a virtual team can be made up of a group of individual sales people who recruit customers and service clients. This does not always guarantee a smooth operation. The most common failings of the virtual team concept often arise from the following negative factors:

- lack of understanding of what virtual teams and remote working is all about
- poor support and commitment by senior management
- inadequate training and development of those who have to work remotely (this is especially true of communications training)
- lack of equipment to do the job properly (technical tools, PCs, mobile phones, etc.)
- lack of technical support and technical training
- failure of the organization to address the issues of virtual teams as part of its own culture change management.

PREREQUISITES FOR INTRODUCING REMOTE TEAM WORKING

Like any new change initiative introduced to the organization, the setting up of virtual teams within the organization should be accompanied by a degree of strategic planning. In effect, this means a re-examination of the organization's goals. The following checklist of questions to ask may be useful.

Checklist of Questions

- Why do we need virtual teams?
- What purpose will they serve?
- Which part of the organization do we have to transform to virtual team working?
- How will their effectiveness be linked to our corporate/organization strategy or strategic goals?
- Who will lead/co-ordinate and/or manage these teams?
- How will we maintain the links between virtual team activity and the mainstream operation?
- What resources (financial, technical, material and human) do we need?
- What support (HR, recruitment, training, finance, engineering, and information technology) will we need?
- How will the establishment of virtual teams affect our:
  - customers
  - suppliers
  - internal systems (administration)?
- What potential is there to involve our competitors and other external agencies in the way we work (remotely)?

Establishing virtual teams

The ideal way to establish virtual teams is to operate in a green field site. Most organizations do not have this privilege. Most often, virtual teams are made to operate in a brown field site, where necessity or business growth has created the phenomenon.

Let us first of all examine the process for setting up a virtual team in a green field site. This will give us some idea of what is ideally possible.

It is important to disseminate information about the big picture and virtual teams to the whole organization.

1. Articulate and share the vision. It is important to disseminate information about the big picture and virtual teams to the whole organization. People need to know why there is a move to virtual teams, what they are for, how they will operate and how they will affect everyday life in the organization. This is as important for staff as for customers and suppliers.

2. Manage the culture change. The switch to virtual teams or remote working may need to be treated as part of a general culture change in the organization. If this is the case, then the leaders and managers may have to commission a cultural needs analysis which looks at the existing management culture. This can be achieved by internal or external consultants depending on how much change management is needed. In some organizations, like Unisys where whole departments were dissolved and reconstructed as virtual teams, there was a major requirement for a formal approach to managing the change. Where possible, staff should be consulted to gain buy in.

3. Link the strategic plan to operational objectives. There has to be a sense of logic about why virtual teams are being set up. The more fact-based these objectives are, the more acceptance and understanding there will be. Most people in traditional operational jobs will be highly suspicious of the concept of virtual teams. They are often seen as flavour of the month fads initiated by interested parties such as information technology lobbyists. The linking of key objectives to the rationale of virtual teams reinforces the basic principles of teamworking – the sharing of common goals.

4. Set up a project management approach. This alleviates the danger of things happening in a reactive or haphazard way. The project management approach to setting up virtual teams guarantees that the outcomes and results of the virtual teams' efforts will be more successful. In addition, the concepts of *Kaizen* can be applied – especially in using some of the *Kaizen* tools such as the *Ishikawa* seven* for analysis and problem solving. This focuses on setting up an infrastructure, time constraints and clear boundaries to define how, who and when work should be completed. In effect, the project management approach is proactive and not reactive. It provides the virtual team with a 'template' for managing its activity which can be referred to by any of the players or team leaders.

5. Recruit a project manager/co-ordinator. This is an important stage when setting up virtual teams. The project manager/co-ordinator should be someone who has experience and a clear understanding of how virtual teams work. Above all, this individual should have above average communication and influencing skills. He or she will be tasked with the

---

* The seven problem-solving tools devised by Dr. Kaoru Ishikawa. These tools facilitate the *Kaizen* practice of Root Cause Analysis.

challenge of operating as a champion of change, a catalyst or change agent who must operate internally and externally and remove obstacles that get in the way of progress. These obstacles could be technical or human. Later on in this chapter, we will describe the process and tasks which the virtual team leader must undertake in order to establish the groundwork for effective team working.

6. Recruit and select the right team players. Again, here we are looking for individuals with a natural ability to communicate. When Sony chose to site their factory in Wales, they did so because of the natural gift of the local Bridge End inhabitants. The local culture was steeped in a tradition of groupworking and community living. Teamworking and communication came naturally to newly recruited Sony workers. With virtual team members, almost 80 per cent of their effectiveness lies in the ability to communicate. This is especially important for blind communication where team members actually cannot see each other. Although much of this communication requires specific training, it helps to recruit people who have a natural aptitude to communicate well.

7. Conduct a training needs analysis. This is similar to any auditing approach. It may be performed by someone from the Human Resources department or by the prospective co-ordinator or project manager. The audit can be conducted against the audit form (opposite).

8. Conduct a technical resources analysis. This requires a similar approach and varies according to different organizations' needs. The most important reason for getting this clearly established and accurately assessed has to do with senior management's approval and commitment. A proactive approach will allow the newly set up virtual team to benefit at the start from getting the correct equipment and resources. It is much more difficult to add to the needs list when the virtual team has commenced operating. Senior management will always view this as extra-budgetary. Where possible it is advisable to gain the advice of unbiased specialists to help identify technical requirements.

9. Set the budget. Once all the groundwork has been done, the job of drafting a feasible budget and indeed acquiring the necessary capital investment will be facilitated. Most virtual teams are not set up this way. They tend to happen quite randomly and are subject to waste and unnecessary spending. This does not meet with the approval of those who control the purse strings. Financial approvers will be more likely to back requests and support the quest of virtual teams in general if they are given specific guidelines to work with.

Skill	Level of competence required	Training required
Telephone skills	High	Formal course
Remote customer handling skills	High	Formal course
Listening skills	High	Formal course
Influencing skills (assertiveness)	High	Formal course
Team skills	High	Formal course
Coaching skills	High	Formal course
Customer relations	High	Formal course
Managing conflict	High	Formal course
Administration	High	Formal course
PC literacy	High	Formal course
Working with intranets and Internet	High	Formal course
Technical problem solving	Average	In-house coaching
Problem solving and decision making	High	Formal course and coaching
Remote team skills	High	Formal course and coaching
Delegation skills	High	Formal course and coaching
Ability to lead and manage outside support resources (including suppliers)	Average	Formal course and coaching
Written communication (e-mail, remote messaging, reports and financial reporting)	High	Formal course and coaching
Basic self-management	High	Formal course and coaching

10. Draft a clear and accurate plan for training and implementation.
This is all part of the 'common sense' approach to setting up virtual teams. Because there is so little precedent associated with setting up and running virtual teams, the more evidence there is of groundwork and infrastructure, the more likelihood there is of gaining full top management support and commitment. Also, the whole concept of virtual teams lends itself to a climate of poor self-discipline. Participants in any virtual team programme need to be able to demonstrate that they are organized and well co-ordinated in everything they do.

Case Study

A large international chemical giant in Europe 'decentralized' in the mid '90s. The idea was to flatten the organization and move control away from the south-east of England into a number of centres in Europe. All this was planned on paper. The Chief Executive and his team were not computer literate. They had little control over the information technology department of their business. As a result, they failed to brief the IT department effectively. The entire project was under-resourced. Only remote team members were given laptops and e-mail or Internet access. As a result, these people could not communicate with their colleagues, clients and suppliers, causing lags in the transfer of essential information. Because there was no clear-cut strategy or proper planning, each locality resourced its own individual needs. Incompatible IT systems and equipment further contributed to lost revenue and inefficiency. This eventually led to a complete reversal of the CEO's policy. He was forced to take back control of the business from the company headquarters in the UK.

Leading and 'working' the virtual team

Once the decision has been made to launch a virtual team, it is important to consider the differences between working with a remote group of individuals who are located in different places and who may work at different times from each other, and a normal conventional team. The following table helps to clarify these differences.

Conventional Team	Virtual Team
Same place, same time zone	Different place, often different time zone
Accessible most of the time	Need to pre-plan access
Regular face-to-face communication	Sporadic face-to-face communication
Lots of informal networking	Informal networking takes place only rarely, when scheduled
Free access to supervision and help	Limited access to help and supervision

Conventional Team	Virtual Team
More time and less pressure to complete tasks	Less time and more pressure to get things done in tightly-framed work schedule
Team players are less conscious of how they communicate and with whom they communicate	Virtual team players have to be very aware of how they come across to others. They must also spend more time planning for communication

THE ROLE OF THE VIRTUAL TEAM LEADER

The role of the virtual team leader (or project manager/co-ordinator) is the very key to the team's growth and success. At the initial stages of the virtual team's development, the team leader must adopt an almost autocratic style in the way he or she leads the team. The main reason for this is so that a culture of self-discipline and respect for boundaries is engendered. Without this commitment, a virtual team may become doomed to fail. As time evolves, the strength of the team leader's style may change. He or she must adopt a less controlling approach. The role of the team leader may be rotated. In some instances, the leadership of the team can even come from a remote source in one of the remote locations. The virtual team leader's checklist opposite contains essential information on how to lead the virtual team.

1. Team leader meets each virtual team player. Once the virtual team has been selected and members have been put in place, the team leader should meet with each individual. This should take place at the most convenient location for both parties. Sometimes it is easier for the team leader to move around the locations. This avoids remote team players having to leave their work sites. The purpose of these meetings is to establish a better understanding of each team player's needs. This meeting also provides the team leader with an opportunity to provide all the necessary information about the virtual team's objectives.

2. Team leader 'audits' the needs of the team and individual players. As part of the initial contact with each member of the virtual team, the team leader can conduct an informal assessment of the team's needs. He or she will have more helicopter vision by virtue of being able to travel from location to location. This provides valuable information and acts as a baseline for developing the team.

Virtual Team Leader's Checklist

- Leader audits the needs of the team and individual players.
- Team leader identifies the strengths and weaknesses of the team.
- Team leader arranges a face-to-face team building session at a mutually accessible location.
- Team leader conducts forum and team brief.
- Team leader arranges training and coaching.
- Team leader agrees achievable goals and measurable objectives with each team member.
- Team leader follows up all contact with secondary communication – e-mail.
- Team leader plans interim 'remote' reviews and three to six month face-to-face reviews.
- Team leader organizes regular face-to-face team get-togethers at a business centre or head office.

3. Team leader identifies the strengths and weaknesses of the team. During these informal encounters, the team leader should be operating as an internal consultant. He or she should adopt a template, e.g. a SWOT analysis in assessing the team. These recorded observations can then be used to work on individual and team development.

4. Team leader arranges a face-to-face team building session at a mutually accessible location. This is a very important part of the virtual team's induction process. Because virtual team players work remotely, they must use every opportunity for face-to-face communication to build a sense of trust and loyalty. The skill and creativity of such a team-building session must be combined with a sense of sharing the common goals and objectives of the team. Individual team players should be encouraged to spend at least ten minutes with every other team player. These one-to-one sessions should be formally structured so that each person goes through a similar process of exchanging information about their work.

The atmosphere of such sessions should be very positive and social without threatening any of the more sensitive personalities. Team leaders should avoid physically strenuous outdoor development activities in case these create a sense of one-upmanship.

Teambuilding sessions may also include the challenge of breaking down barriers between remote team players. The old saying: 'You never get a second chance to make a first impression' is particularly true when it comes to remote working. It is difficult enough to remove these barriers in a team where people are working face to face. This is even more daunting with virtual teams. Virtual team players are far more likely to ignore people they don't feel comfortable with, especially if those people represent a different discipline, function or even nationality. In international organizations it is essential for the team leader to address cross-cultural misunderstanding.

Case Study

A major multinational US chemical company on the East Coast recently became involved in a joint venture with a German counterpart. Four or five groups of people in Germany and Pennsylvania were meant to work together in virtual cross-functional teams. The Americans knew nothing about working with Germans although the Germans had a lot more experience in dealing with Americans. The American project manager responsible for setting up the teams commissioned a consultant and expert on cross-cultural relationships to run a briefing session in the United States. The session proved invaluable, as most of the Americans had had little exposure to the way German managers ran their businesses. This was particularly important in terms of understanding the German team approach and autocratic management styles. The sessions allowed better empathy and tolerance to develop between both sides.

---

5. Team leader conducts forum and team brief. As mentioned, the team building sessions offer a unique opportunity for the team leader to present himself or herself to the team. In addition the team leader should also use the occasion to communicate with the team by presenting the latest news and information concerning the organization, the team and its objectives. Sometimes this may be done through video conferencing. This is especially useful where remote players are scattered across the globe.

6. Team leader arranges training and coaching. A key function of the team leader is to identify and arrange training or coaching for the team. This may include team training – leading to remote team awareness and specific team skills including some team games which help to demonstrate the power and importance of good communication to a virtual team. Especially important is the inclusion of training that emphasizes how to enhance communication and interpersonal skills when individuals are working blindly, i.e. they cannot see each other. This is not only important amongst team players, it affects every relationship where people are using remote tools such as the telephone or the Internet. There is even a special requirement for teaching video conferencing skills. This is a new form of technology that is becoming less costly. Most new personal computers are being fitted with miniature cameras and microphones. New software allows video conferencing from an office desktop. While this sounds exciting, the equipment needs to be used effectively with a degree of training and coaching.

7. Team leader agrees achievable goals and measurable objectives with each team member. One of the main enemies of the virtual team culture is rampant individualism! Because virtual team players are often left to themselves to get on with their work, they may often choose to focus on what they like to do as opposed to what is necessary or important for the team. In this regard, it is important for the team leader to agree clear targets made up of goals and specific objectives. The more quantifiable these objectives, the better. Team players should be given the opportunity to express their views and question the objectives. They should also be allowed to focus on creative objectives that encourage them to take an innovative and creative approach to their work.

8. Team leader follows up all contact with secondary communication – e-mail. Once again, because of the distracting nature of remote working, there is a need to constantly reinforce messages and communication. This may be achieved by e-mail, voice mail and faxes. Modern communication technology helps to ensure that messages aren't ignored. Many desktop and laptop PCs have a facility where e-mail pops up onto a screen and is not removed until the message is acknowledged or dealt with. The use of infrared palmtop technology now makes it easier for team players to pass on information to each other without using a keyboard. Everything is moving towards quicker, simpler action.

The concept of remote coaching can be added to the coaching process. This is where the team leader conducts a regular exchange of e-mail. The virtual team player is given an opportunity of sharing some of his or her challenges with the team leader and/or colleagues. This promotes joint problem solving and builds on the establishment of a climate of trust.

Case Study

An international software company based in the UK Midlands instituted a remote coaching programme within the team. Virtual team players are encouraged to send e-mail questions and answers to one another. The following is an example of such e-mail exchanges.

13 January 99 – For the attention of GF:
I was to get back to you about progress I had made with tasks since we had last met, which I will now do:
(one thing – I thought you were going to send me a document which could be used to review meeting performance – especially with TS).
I would claim that with respect to some of the points, that the opportunity has not presented itself since we met. Into this would fall:

- *use more active listening skills to clarify when faced with a passive person and especially on the phone*
- *look for external speaking opportunities to strengthen my confidence.*

For managing SB – I am giving him more praise
(though I have to be careful here as he tries it on sometimes if he thinks I am over sympathetic) I am also trying to use more open questions – think he is responding slowly to this (takes a bit of getting used to).

For managing PB – certainly I have encouraged him to do informal interviews and have suggested means of getting feedback – I do feel he is improving in this respect. Being more task oriented with him – I must admit I have not done that yet.

In general, with both, I am seeing slow but steady progress. To some extent that could be my fault with finding more time.
In terms of prioritizing my own time, I did a bit of work on that but I need to do more to really do it justice – a matter of finding a quiet hour.

That's about it really, did others feed back to you? In general I have not done as much as I should and I am focusing more on the management of others than myself. I have noted an action to re-examine my own priorities in the next month.

Jon.

9. Team leader plans interim 'remote' reviews and three to six month face-to-face reviews. This procedure is part of the team leader's skill in making sure that the team remains on target. This provides the team with an opportunity to examine its progress. These sessions must be advertised well in advance so that all attendees can plan ahead and mark the occasion in their diaries. Nowadays, this is facilitated by the use of electronic diaries. Virtual team players are linked through electronic networks and team leaders can access this data to select the most appropriate dates. Information about the team should be published regularly. Process review and renewed process mapping may form part of the team's self-styled *Kaizen* or continuous improvement culture. Some companies have established a reward scheme which is published on an intranet website – where team players can access information about the team's progress. This plays a vital part in keeping the team focused. Where the entire team cannot meet up face to face, the team leader may have to conduct the reviews with smaller groups of people made up of different clusters of team players. Where it is impossible to meet face to face with the whole team or segments of the team, then these reviews must be conducted remotely – preferably using technology such as video conferencing. This allows more visual exposure to data including graphs, charts or even concrete material – a virtual tour of an office or factory site to show remote team players the three dimensional layout of a proposed new worksite.

10. Team leader organizes regular face-to-face team get-togethers. Most virtual team experiences are not without problems. The key to solving these problems is face-to-face review and evaluation. No matter how sophisticated the world of business becomes, 80 per cent of employed staff acknowledge that face-to-face communication is best. Virtual teams can build on the fact that 'absence makes the heart grow fonder'. Motivation and renewed enthusiasm are a direct by-product of the reconvened team. This is not only to be recommended, it may also be a crucial part of the team's survival. Another great counter-force in the stability of virtual teams is change. As the new millennium approaches, organizations are experiencing more radical change. Recent mega mergers and take-overs have made a massive impact on teams. Just when a team has welded itself together, organizational changes can rip the team apart, forcing team players to move on, or to become redeployed elsewhere in the organization. This is even more true of virtual teams who by their very nature are more vulnerable. Their structure and

> *No matter how sophisticated the world of business becomes, 80 per cent of employed staff acknowledge that face-to-face communication is best.*

stability is far more fragile. Any impending change or restructuring can only be managed by careful handling accompanied by more face-to-face contact with as many of the virtual stakeholders as possible.

SUMMARY

In this chapter we have looked at the prerequisites for setting up virtual teams. We have taken into account all the planning that is necessary to make virtual teams work. We have also taken into account the tools, both technical and managerial, that are necessary for the implementation of virtual team work. We have discussed the advantages and pitfalls of virtual teams. Finally we have put forward some practical guidelines for how to lead and manage these teams. Much of what is contained in this chapter reflects the general ethos of normal team working. The virtual team requires a far more intense and sensitive approach. This is particularly true of the communication factor. In ordinary team working, a great deal can be assumed and taken for granted. In virtual teams, assumptions and uncorroborated interpretations of others' behaviour are potentially disastrous. The virtual team approach is analogous with creating a tapestry. The right equipment is crucial – hardware, software and the development of a systematic framework for communication is vital. Added to this are the components of people and their skills like the different stitching in colourful needlework. Each piece of thread is important in how it is linked to the next. Although some stitches are not directly linked, their effect is crucial to the grand design. When one stands back from the loom, one begins to see how the strands of thread and stitches come together to give the work meaning and impact. The same is true of a well-crafted virtual team.

CHAPTER 12

Future Teams and Implications

Introduction

———

Global Business Trends

———

The Challenges and Changes of
Developing Technologies

———

Becoming a Continuous Learning Team

———

How to Teambuild for the Future

———

Summary

ALAN M. BARRATT

Associate, Europe Japan Centre

ALAN BARRATT OUTLINES THE DRIVERS of modern organizational change
and suggests how they will affect the future of teams. He looks at the
effect of communications technology on teams, and deals also with
group dynamics and the need for continuous learning in teams. He
demonstrates the use of the Margerison McCann model of psychological typology as a contribution to team building.

INTRODUCTION

Since the dawn of reason the majority of the human race has been fearful of the future, or at best has a high level of anxiety. The speed of
business changes is accelerating at a rate never previously dreamed about.
However, the business community, although well aware of the impact of
business changes, learns slowly from each other and is rarely proactive in
the implementation of paradigm shifts and new business practices.

This chapter takes a look at global business trends and the impact
on teams by examining the following:

- what teams need to do to remain high performing
- the challenges of developing and changing technologies
- key strategies to become the continuously learning team
- how to teambuild for the future
- the future psychological impact on individual team members
- the critical actions to achieve high performance teams for the future.

GLOBAL BUSINESS TRENDS

The widely available variety of concepts, approaches, best practices,
latest ideas and new pronouncements from gurus must have most business people in a state of shell-shock, so let us take a simple perspective
of the global trends that are impacting many businesses today. If you are
in the service or manufacturing industries these trends will be clearly
recognized in your business to a greater or lesser extent.

Ask directors, managers or supervisors what in the workplace is
dramatically different from 10 or 20 years ago and the answer will probably go something like this:

> *We are working under increased pressure, harder, longer hours with less resources than we need. We are trying to cope with huge changes in structure, technology, business demands and competition. Everyone wants results yesterday. The effect is that stress levels for us are dangerously high and not consistent with the rewards provided.*

Let us take a look at some of the trends impacting business today.

1. **Size** of the organization seems to be out of fashion, but **speed** is certainly in. Having said that, in many industries, we are seeing large multinationals merging together to compete in the global marketplace. Examples are the oil industry and the partnership arrangements in the airline business. But few companies would disagree that speed is the driving factor.

2. **Stability** in organizations is out, **change** is in. Many of us are dealing with such a variety of changes that we are convinced we will never see stability again. But our grandparents probably felt exactly the same way in the early part of the twentieth century.

3. Organizational **hierarchies** are out, or at least dramatically flattened, but **teams** as business units are in. The traditional organizational pyramid has been changing for the last two decades. Instead the practice of managers leading complex matrix teams working on cross-functional projects has become commonplace. Teams are business focused on specific improvement projects, often in a *Kaizen* environment. Total quality, customer focus groups, challenge task forces, best practice implementation are common areas of focus.

4. **Customer service** is out, but **customer driven processes** are in. The 1980s and 90s saw heightened awareness and considerable effort placed on customer service, giving the customer a level of service which was perceived as required – this was a move forward. Now the focus has moved towards the customer telling us what service-related business processes we need to put in place to meet their needs and expectations.

5. Business **structure around function** is out, however, **structure around products** and services is in. Smaller profit-centred structures are critical to today's highly competitive global marketplace. If companies today wish to be successful they must move fast and manage change as if it was second nature. This is only possible with a dynamic, proactive small team which is highly focused, and motivated towards clear goals and results. Small is clearly beautiful.

If companies today wish to be successful they must move fast and manage change as if it was second nature.

BECOMING A
CONTINUOUS LEARNING TEAM

When we pick up any management book or article today, we read about the importance of the continuous learning process. There is little doubt that learning is becoming critical in the information age. In fact it is possible that we are learning at a faster rate today than ever before.

Great teams make just as many mistakes as poor teams, but great teams learn more quickly from their mistakes and do not keep repeating the same mistake time after time.

There appear to be two key issues that impact teams for the future to make them successful as learning teams.

- The team's ability to learn and become skilled in new and changing technologies and their competence in transferring those technologies to others who need to know.

- The team's drive to learn from mistakes they make and how they internalize that learning for the future. The research on teams show that great teams make just as many mistakes as poor teams, but great teams learn more quickly from their mistakes and do not keep repeating the same mistake time after time.

Let us look at these two key points in more depth.

Learning and transferring new technologies

Critical to business success is the careful acquisition of appropriate technologies, selecting the near-perfect fit against current and future applications. Within any team at least one team member should champion the technology, become the new paradigm pioneer, taking responsibility for ensuring all other team members are aware and appropriately skilled. That champion would provide a focus for emerging new technologies that would help the team by playing the team role of the information collector.

Critical to any success is the effective technology implementation or transfer of technology. This process is often poorly conducted and can dilute the potential benefits of any technology. Ten years ago I published in MCB's Top Management Digest[1] an article outlining the technology transfer process which argued that transferring technology is very similar to the selling/influencing process and needs to be taken seriously if the organization wishes to take any technological competitive advantage.

Great teams adopt the right technologies and transfer them across the team effectively.

Great teams adopt the right technologies and transfer them across the team effectively.

Reviewing the team's performance

The second expertise that a great team must develop is the ability to honestly and openly review their performance effectiveness. A regular exercise for any team, which will become more critical in the future, is to look at itself and learn some lessons, both from successes and failures, and internalize those learning points.

Some key questions team members might ask themselves are as follows.

- Which factors are really making our team perform?
- Which factors are hindering our success?
- Are we communicating effectively enough, both within the team and to all our clients? (That means all other interfaces.)
- Could the team's dynamics and interpersonal relationships be improved?
- Are the team's goals of output and quality being achieved?
- Is there sufficient mutual respect and trust in the team?
- Are all the team members coping with the current technologies?
- Is the team motivated and having fun?

We all can count on one issue: that technology will keep developing and changing and all teams will be challenged to cope with the implications. Clearly, high performing teams must be on top of technologies that will help them, ensure that effective technology transfer takes place, and they must regularly review their team's performance by holding up that mirror and realistically addressing those key questions.

Finally, great teams are well aware of how their team compares with others within their own organization and if they are really tuned in they will compare themselves to external teams, i.e. within the industry, their profession and their country, through best practice data, surveys or informal networks.

HOW TO TEAMBUILD
FOR THE FUTURE

There are as many different approaches to teambuilding as there are products on the shelves of your local superstore. Many are successful and just as many can be dysfunctional to the team and organization. In my own consulting practice as much as 20–25 per cent of my teambuilding is remedial. By that I mean some other organization or consultants have worked with the client, with unsuccessful results, and called me in to have another go to achieve success. So let me share with you my approach to teambuilding for the future.

In my opinion, successful teambuilding is based on some pragmatic assumptions.

1. Team members must have a deep understanding of each other.
2. Teams must focus specifically on the future (in a planned way like a business/profit plan, e.g. detailed for the next 12 months and more generally for years 2 and 3).
3. Communication improvements and anticipated technology changes should be factored in.
4. The team's critical success factors should be identified, prioritized and specific detailed action plans developed.
5. All team members should champion appropriate tracks of the action plans and make commitments to deliver results on time.

My experience has shown that teambuilding is a process, not an event, which means that it should start with some goals, expectations and deliverables followed by an appropriate diagnosis, and a teambuilding design that produces results and agreed deliverables. Little and often seems to work more effectively.

Today's challenges are with teams whose members do not meet face to face and with whom a teambuilding process has to be orchestrated through technology.

Today's challenges are with teams whose members do not meet face to face and with whom a teambuilding process has to be orchestrated through technology. However, the same assumptions as outlined above need to be realized, whether through a team seminar, videoconference or distance learning via Internet or intranet.

A typical teambuilding design for coping with the team's future might have subject areas as follows.

Subject Areas for Teambuilding Design

- objectives, expectations and deliverables
- obtaining a deep understanding of you and the rest of your team:
  - the synolic model
  - teambuilding technology
  - personal profiles to identify work preferences (Myers-Briggs, PPI, Belbin, Disc, or, my preferred profiling system, Margerison/McCann[2] TMS)
- the characteristics of high performance teams
- understanding the balance of teams and options for improvement
- planning the integration and communication processes within the team
- establishing the team's vision, goals and values
- team leader's executive input (if appropriate)
- planning and projecting ahead the team's results:
  - brainstorming the current issues, challenges for the future
  - identifying the critical success factors (CSF) for the team over the next 6–12 months
  - prioritizing the CSFs for rapid organizational impact
- develop specific action plans for each CSF
- make personal commitments to champion individual tracts from the action plan
- agree next steps and how the team will monitor its action plans.

This design has worked in many parts of the world, is culturally accepted everywhere, can be delivered in many different ways, from a seminar format to an intranet teleconference configuration. It is a basic design which can be expanded, with many subject additions, reflecting the team's needs and the pre-design diagnosis.

As many teams in the future will be put together on the basis of solving organizational issues, team members will be performing in not one, but several teams, some of which are likely to be outside their normal structural role. From this assumption, it will be critical, for all individuals, to develop a high level of team playing skills.

Individuals who prefer to be sole contributors (my experience suggests they are in the order of 1 in 7) will be presented with a difficult challenge by the increased emphasis on teamworking. For the team leaders, the strategy will be to select a well-defined role with a single point reporting contact. Alternatively an adjunct role might be appropriate, reporting and contributing into the team. The individual sole contributor needs to negotiate his or her role and contributions very specifically with the team, so that the complete team is clear on what to expect from the individual.

Most team purists would urge sole contributors to become full team members or to find another role. In reality, we must find ways around this problem, and maximize the talents and preferences of the individual.

The psychological impact on team members in the future

Teams in the future will be under more pressure to succeed, and will be more complex to operate to achieve full synergy.

Technology and strategic organizational changes will create further stress for the team and particularly for individual team members. So what are the specific areas that individuals will need to be proactively aware of, and what actions need to be taken to compensate?

I mentioned earlier in this chapter that there are many teambuilding technologies that provide team members with a depth of knowledge of themselves and others. Using the Margerison/McCann[2] model (Fig. 12.1 overleaf), which is my preference, I want to illustrate the actions individuals need to stress, through certain behaviours, to contribute more positively to the workings of their team.

In this model, the spectrum of behaviour (e.g. Extrovert/Introvert) is shown for categories of team or individual activities.

Table 12.2 opposite outlines the awareness needed and possible actions to take to improve individual contribution to a high performing team.

Hopefully, it will give you some guidelines or helpful tips on the role you prefer to play within the team. Assess which characteristics are clearly you, then try some of the suggested actions to see if they can help the team as a whole.

Of course, this is just part of the picture, every other team member should examine their preferences in a similar way and adjust their behaviours to contribute to that high performance team.

Figure 12.1 *Margerison/McCann teambuilding model*

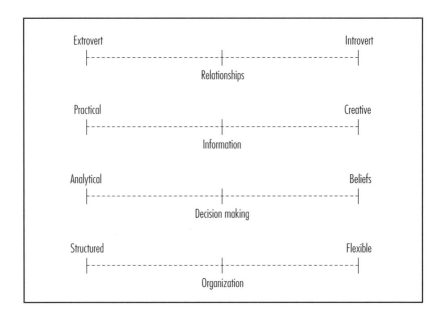

Table 12.2 *A checklist of possible behaviour modification*

	Awareness Needed	Actions to Consider
EXTROVERTS	Will think about issues by talking them through.	Let the team know the direction you are heading.
	Enjoy a variety of tasks and activities.	Focus on specific issues particularly in meetings or conference calls, etc.
	Likely to be very vocal meetings/dialogues.	Make clear points and statements and do some active listening.
INTROVERTS	Prefer to think issues out before speaking.	Let team know you are considering this issue in depth before stating your view.
	Like to concentrate on a few tasks at a time.	Let it be known that you like to concentrate on a few and deliver on time.
	Likely to be more quiet at meetings/dialogues.	Make a point of stating two or three key prepared messages at each meeting.
PRACTICAL	Are present-oriented and like to discuss today's reality.	Show the team that the future is important too, but we will not get there unless we focus on today.
	Are patient with routine deliver results.	Some of the team will work and need to recognize your preference is critical to the team's success.
	Usually sound on the details but may not always see the big picture.	Let the team be aware that the details plus the big picture equal team balance.
CREATIVE	Are future oriented.	Let the team know that the future is important to move forward, but the past and present also have an importance.
	Are always searching for new ways and methods.	The team needs to realize we all should be looking for improvements (Kaizen).
	Often see the big picture but may miss the details.	The restatement to the team of the big picture can provide an effective focus and summary.

	Awareness Needed	Actions to Consider
ANALYTICAL	Measure decisions made against payoffs.	Must be perceived by the team as considering the feelings as much as the facts when making decisions.
	Places emphasis on the current situation.	Your team needs to know that you have factored-in the longer term implications of your decision.
	Prefer analysis and clarity.	Recognize that others in your team may have strong beliefs and 'gut feel' which on occasions could prove conflicting.
BELIEFS	Can become overly-committed to a viewpoint.	Realize the impact this can have on your team, you might sound like a broken record on occasions.
	Negotiates on the rights and wrongs of the issues.	You need sometimes to let your team know that the facts and situation are as important as your views and beliefs.
	Are likely to be nostalgic, holding to traditional ways.	The team needs to know from you that the past can be learned from.
STRUCTURED	Are action-oriented and concerned with resolving issues.	You must give time to your team to think issues through before taking action so to obtain full 'buy-in'.
	May rush to quick decisions without sufficient information.	Involve your teams in getting the facts/data where possible.
	Are reluctant to change once a judgement is made.	Show the team that you are not rigid in your style, but change for change's sake can be dysfunctional.
FLEXIBLE	Are prone to information overload which can delay decisions.	Obtain the support of the team to drive the agreed deadlines forward and don't drown under the paper/data.
	Often appear disorganized.	Let the team know that they should not be misled by what appears as disorganized, as I keep the structure in my head.
	Regularly place emphasis on diagnosing over concluding and resolving.	Let your team know that to me it is important to study the issue in depth, sometimes to the point of paralysis, before deciding on actions.

SUMMARY

A summary of the critical team actions/issues for the future.

- Recognize the rapid speed of change.
- Be aware of the global trends in business, the impact on your team, and the paradigm changes in your industry.
- Set aggressive team goals and be attentive to the changing roles within teams in the future, and clarify regularly.
- Assess the impact of new technologies on the team and how team performance is affected.
- Set up an appropriate communication system within the team and monitor its effectiveness.
- Expect a dramatic heightening of the importance of group dynamic and interpersonal relationships with the team, as technology and electronics take hold.
- Develop a learning team that really reviews its performance and lessons learned and continuously grows.
- More teambuilding and team development activities will be required, designed creatively for the future.
- The future team will need to have a greater awareness of the psychological impact each team member will have on each other. This means:
  - recognizing your own preferences
  - understanding the preferences of others.

  The actions to consider are not just to tolerate other people's differences but to 'treasure' them to the extent that they add real value to you and your team.

In these turbulent times we all can choose to be pulled along by the tide of change, or be part of the change movement, by planning and championing change for the future.

The choice is entirely yours.

Notes

1. Barratt, Alan M. (1989) 'Technology Transfer,' *Top Management Digest*, MCB University Press, Vol. 1

2. Margerison, C.J. and McCann, D.J. (1990) *Team Management*, Mercury Books

GLOSSARY

Business Process Reengineering
A system developed by Michael
Hammer which examines all the
processes that take place as work flows
through an organization. The system
then seeks to eliminate all redundant or
non-value-adding activities and
processes thus saving cost.

Electronic Cottage   The phrase is
used to summarize the idea of an
organization in which employees work
from home rather than on company
premises. All employees are linked
together by electronic communications
systems and networks.

Gemba   Literally 'the place where it
happens' but actually meaning where
work is actually done, i.e. on a
production line, in a company
department, etc.

Gembutsu   The tangible objects at
Gemba, e.g. finished or part finished
products or components, the machines
used, the components stored to perform
the process, etc.

Generation X employee   A phrase
used to describe people born after the
1960s – the youngest generation of
employees who are reputed not to
expect permanent lifetime employment,
are interested in the employer offering
development opportunities and who
expect a varied working life and career.

Genjitsu   The actual situation.

Hoshin kanri   Literally policy
management – used to mean 'compass
navigation' but actually a planning
system which establishes clear goals and
destinations and seeks to gain employee
alignment to help achieve goals.

Kaizen   Literally change and good;
continuous improvement – actually a
whole philosophy of employee
standards and team working based on
the belief that everything is capable of
improvement.

Kanban   A Kanban is literally a chit
or slip of plastic placed in a bin of
inventory which when it becomes
visible indicates that supplies need
renewal. It is then passed back to the
inventory source for replenishment. The
significance of kanban however is the
automatic and timely replacement of
inventory so that the process of
manufacture is not interrupted.

Karoshi   Death by stress caused by
over-work.

Muda   Literally waste; identifying and
eliminating waste.

Seiketsu   Clean regularly; systematize.

Seiri   Clear out and eliminate
unnecessary things; sort.

Seiso   Make sure environment is completely clean; scrub.

Seiton   Make materials readily accessible; straighten.

Shitsuke   Do processes regularly and improve them continually; standardize.

Total Quality Management TQM
Managerial and process systems which an organization adopts or imposes upon itself to assure that all its activities conform to specified standards at all times.

INDEX